Giuseppe Marco Antonio Baretti

A Journey From London to Genoa

Through England, Portugal, Spain and France

Giuseppe Marco Antonio Baretti

A Journey From London to Genoa
Through England, Portugal, Spain and France

ISBN/EAN: 9783744761710

Printed in Europe, USA, Canada, Australia, Japan

Cover: Foto ©Andreas Hilbeck / pixelio.de

More available books at **www.hansebooks.com**

A

JOURNEY

FROM

LONDON to GENOA,

THROUGH

ENGLAND, PORTUGAL, SPAIN,

and FRANCE.

By JOSEPH BARETTI,
Secretary for Foreign Correspondence to the Royal
Academy of Painting, Sculpture, and Architecture.

VOL. IV.

LONDON,
Printed for T. DAVIES, in Ruffel-Street, Covent-
Garden; and L. DAVIS, in Holborn.
MDCCLXX.

LETTER LXX.

Deſarts not frightful. A Nota Bene *and a* Digreſſion. *Fine faces in Biſcay. Great coquettes. Knowledge of languages in women.* Landes *of* Bourdeaux. Pais de Bigorre. Filles Gaſconnes *and* Filles Baſquoiſes. *Biſcayans, not beggars, and why. Many of them at* Madrid. *They retire to their country. Not ſo the gentry of Scotland and Savoy. Well-looking houſes in Biſcay. Dialects of the* Baſcuenze. Laramendi's *works.* Baſcuenze-*library ſmall enough. An Iriſh merchant at* Bilbao. *Terrifying hills. Wiſdom of mules. Town of* Orduña, *Peña of* Orduña, *and river* Orduña. *Iron Manufactories.* Cha-colin

colin *of* Serraos. *A tool like an* H, *and its use.* Lino, *Turkey-corn, goats-cheese and milk, small cattle, few sheep, and good pork. Trees annually planted.* Angullas. Orduña *and* Bilbao's *fine situations. Inconveniencies in Spain. No new edicts, no new laws, no tax-gatherers. Arrival of an Italian singer. The quibbles of Spanish Capuchins.*

Fraga, Oct. 24, 1760.

YESTERDAY we crossed a small desart, and this day another. But do not imagine a Spanish desart to be any thing of the frightful kind, like those of Libia, full of tygers and lions, hyenas and serpents. The desarts of this country are nothing but tracts of land, generally formed of a compact gravel, that produce nothing but rosemary, thyme, sage, rue, spike, and other such odoriferous shrubs, in so great abundance, as to furnish the inhabitants with what

fuel

fuel they want. You may well think, that travelling through fuch tracts, efpecially after a light fhower, as it was my cafe this morning, cannot but prove delightful, becaufe of the fragrance exhaling all around.

Having gone through the two fmall villages of *Peñalba* and *Candafmos*, we ftopped to dine at the *Venta de Fraga*, about five leagues from *Bujalaróz*; then came to fup and fleep at *Fraga*, which is two leagues diftant from that *venta*. Thefe two laft leagues are woody and cultivated, becaufe of the river *Cinque* or *Cinca*, which fends out many ftreams to the right and left.

The pleafantnefs of the road was ftill encreafed by the talk of my friend the Canon, whofe company I like every hour more. As yefterday he had mentioned the principality, or *feigniory*, of Bifcay, and promifed to fay fomething of the language and character of the inhabitants, I put him in mind of it. What follows

follows is the substance of what I learned of him upon this subject.

N. B. Some years after the date of these letters (as I said in another place) I went a second time to Madrid, and took *Biscay* and *Navarre* in my way. To make a long stay in either was not in my power: yet I neglected not to observe well the land I crossed, and informed myself of the language and manners of the inhabitants as accurately, as a slow journey on a mule would permit, besides tarrying one day in one place, and another in another, wherever I thought that a short stop might be conducive to my being apprised of any thing worth the telling. My reader therefore must give me leave to sink the account I had from the *Canon of Siguenza*, and take in the stead the following

DIGRESSION.

' The people of Biscay and Navarre
' are in general as well limbed as any
' of the petty nations that live on
' our Apennines: yet no where on the
' Apennines have I seen so many hand-
' some women as in Biscay, where almost
' every posada offered at least one beau-
' tiful face; nor have I as yet forgotten
' three

'three sisters at *Ortéz* [a small town
'about four leagues from *Pampeluna*]
'whom I thought worth a kingdom
'a-piece. 'Tis pity however, that the
'sex throughout Biscay have the reputa-
'tion of being the arrantest coquettes in
'the world. Besides my own observa-
'tions on their general character, I have
'been told by their own men in the
'jollity of converse, that most women
'throughout the seigniory will ogle, and
'whisper, and smile, and flatter, and
'elbow slily, and squeeze your hand, to
'draw a present from you if possible,
'and without intending the least return.
'Both the married and unmarried will
'thus endeavour to trick any traveller.

'Many Biscayan women of the lower
'sort, while very young, go to service
'in the neighbouring provinces, where
'their habiliment and hair-dress, prettily
'peculiar, render them distinguishable
'at the first glance. There are numbers
'of them at *Bayonne*, and throughout
'the

' the *Païs* * *de Bigorre*. I cannot for-
' bear to tell, that at an inn of *Bayonne*,
' where I stopped three or four days, I
' met with two Biscayan maids, who,
' besides their own *Bascuenze*, could
' speak, and very intelligibly, the *French*
' and *Spanish*, together with the *Gascoon*
' *dialect* that is spoken there, and under-
' stood throughout the *Landes* of *Bour-*
' *deaux* and the *Païs de Bigorre*. The
' necessity that forces the females of Bis-
' cay to know more than one language,
' is far from impairing their beauty, as
' no new language can be learned with-
' out acquiring new ideas; and the more
' ideas a woman has, the more agreeable

---

* *The French call* Païs de Bigorre *a tract of country which lies between the* Landes de Bourdeaux *and the* Pirenees. *The* Landes *of* Bourdeaux *are divided into* Grandes Landes *and* Petites Landes. *The* Grandes *extend almost from Bourdeaux to Bayonne one way, and the* Petites *another way, still between those two towns. Both the* Grandes *and* Petites Landes *are sandy tracts scarcely inhabited: yet the* Petites *are less barren than the* Grandes.

' she

'she will be. But the Biscayan wenches
' turn their natural, as well as their ac-
' quired powers, to no other purpose but
' that of coquettry, and the more agree-
' able they know themselves to be, the
' more they expect from every man who
' covets their converse; for ever alluring,
' for ever kindling hope, and for ever
' disappointing.

' It is a general custom throughout the
' southern parts of France to have female
' servants at the inns as well as in private
' families; and it is that custom that
' draws into the different parts of *Gas-*
' *cony* and *Guyenne* a multitude of women
' from Biscay, as in both those countries
' they are sure of being preferred to the
' natives by most masters and mistresses.
' The *filles Gasconnes*; that is, the *Gas-*
' *coon female servants*, are in general short
' and clumsy, with broad, tawny, and
' unmeaning faces; whereas the *filles*
' *Basquoises* are almost all of a good size,
' and well shaped, with lively black eyes
' and

' and clear complexions, and a smartness
' about them that is attracting. Then
' the manners of the *Gasconnes* are coarse
' and impudent, and they scruple not to
' throw themselves at once into the power
' of him, who will have them for the
' smallest sum; whereas the *Basquoises* are
' sly and scrupulous, and will go no far-
' ther than wheedling and cajoling, only
' wanting to put together some hundreds
' of livres to go back to their country
' to marry. I must however say, that
' the *filles Basquoises* who resort most to
' the French side of the Pirenees, are for
' the greatest part natives of that tract of
' Biscay which belongs to the crown of
' France. A young woman from Spanish
' Biscay, is not called *fille Basquoise* by
' the French; but *fille Biscayenne*, or
' *fille de la Biscaye*; and these like better
' to go to service in *Navarre* and *Old*
' *Castile*, than in any part of *Guyenne* or
' *Gascony*.

' With

'With regard to the men of Biscay,
'it is commonly said in Spain, as well
'as in France, that they will rather steal
'than beg; not that they are remarkable
'for thieving, but because they scorn
'begging. They have a tradition in
'Biscay, and the other provinces where
'the *Bascuenze* is spoken, that one of
'their ancient kings declared them all
'*Hidalgos*; and this is the reason, that
'no *Biscayan*, *Guipuscoan*, or *Alavan*
'will degrade himself by asking alms.
'This however is not quite the case with
'the *Navarrans*, as you meet in that
'kingdom with many of both sexes,
'who disdain not to beg; but wait for
'you on the high roads, holding up
'wooden crucifixes and saints, which
'they would fain induce you to kiss, as
'it is the practice in several other pro-
'vinces of Spain, most especially Estre-
'madura.

'I have been told, that, proportion of
'extent considered, there are at Madrid
'more

'more natives of Bifcay, than of any
'other Spanifh province; and that no
'Bifcayan goes to feek for an employ-
'ment to that capital, but what is fure
'of finding one. Befides that at Madrid
'the notion is general, that the Bifcayans
'are more knowing and active than other
'Spaniards; the Bifcayans ftand by each
'other vigoroufly wherever they meet
'out of their own province, and pro-
'mote each other's intereft by a kind of
'tacit confederacy. They fay in Eng-
'land, that this is in a good meafure the
'cafe with the Scots; and I know
'that in Piedmont the Savoyards keep
'ftrongly knitted to each other: but as
'foon as the Bifcayans have acquired
'fome fortune at Madrid, they quit the
'place and retire to their own dear
'mountains, and there build themfelves
'good houfes, and live the remainder
'of their days in eafe and comfort;
'whereas the Savoyards, when once
'fettled in Piedmont, think no more of

'the

' the weſtern ſide of Mount Cenis, ex-
' cept they are porters, chimney-ſweep-
' ers, and marmote-ſhowers. Nor is
' the caſe much different with the Scots
' when they have once got root in any
' country, eſpecially in England, where
' moſt of them will do any thing, rather
' than go back to their homes. This is
' at leaſt what every Engliſhman will tell
' you as ſoon as you mention the ſubject;
' and the numbers of Scots to be met
' throughout England do not belie the
' obſervation: but both the Engliſh and
' the Piedmonteſe do honour againſt their
' will both to the Scots and Savoyards
' when they reproach them with their
' ſupporting each other out of their own
' countries. Inſtead of a reproach, I
' take this to be a commendation.

' The perpetual return of the Biſ-
' cayans to the places of their nativity,
' is the cauſe that one ſees, even on
' the rougheſt mountains, a great many
' houſes that are very well built, with
' panes

'panes of glasses to their windows, and
'with neat window-shutters painted yel-
'low or green: a sight that I never had
'in any of the petty towns and villages
'I crossed in various parts of that large
'kingdom, though I travelled little less
'than two thousand miles about it.
'What sort of conveniencies the Bis-
'cayans have within doors, I cannot tell,
'because I have entered very few: yet
'the outward appearance of their houses
'will make any body think favourably
'of the inward.

'The Biscayan language, or *Bascuenze*,
'as they call it, according to the idea
'that I have been able to form of it,
'must be divided at least into three
'dialects; of which the first, or mother-
'tongue, must be called *Biscayan*, the
'second *Navarran*, and the third *Basque*.

'The *Biscayan dialect*, or mother-
'tongue, I take to be that, which is
'spoken through that part of Biscay, the
'inhabitants of which consider the town

'of

'of *Bilbao*, or rather that of *Orduña*, to
' be their capital. The chief feat of this
' dialect, or tongue, I take to be that,
' which is fpoken in either of thofe
' towns, only fix leagues diftant from
' each other.

'The *Navarran dialect* I call that,
' which is fpoken through the beft part
' of the little kingdom of *Navarre*: and
' as *Pampeluna* is the capital of that
' kingdom, it is to be fuppofed that the
' pureft *Navarran* is fpoken at *Pampe-*
' *luna*.

'The *Bafque dialect* I term that, which
' is fpoken through that tract of country,
' called *Païs de Bafque* by the French,
' to whom it belongs. That *Païs* is
' chiefly formed by thirty three villages
' and their territories, all fubject to the
' fpiritual jurifdiction of the bifhoprick
' of *Bayonne*. And as the moft confider-
' able of thofe thirty three villages is *San*
' *Juan de Luz*, there, I fuppofe, the beft
' *Bafque* is fpoken, the chief people of
' the

'the *Païs de Basque* residing in that vil-
'lage, which the French term á *bourg*
'or *ville*, to give it some pre-eminence
'over the rest of those villages.

'I am however sensible that this divi-
'sion of the Biscayan language into three
'principal dialects, or into a mother-
'tongue and two dialects, cannot be
'looked upon as exact. There are the
'speeches of *Guipúscoa* and *A'lava*, which
'seem to have as good a claim to the
'denomination of dialects as the *Na-*
'*varran* and *Basque*, because, like these
'two, they deviate much from the
'mother-tongue, and have some pecu-
'liarities of their own in their respective
'constructions. Nay, father *Laramendi*
'(of whom anon) divides the Biscayan
'tongue into three dialects as well as I;
'but with this material difference, that
'he calls the first *Guipúscoan*, the second
'*Biscayan*, and the third *Navarran*,
'totally omitting the *Basque* and the
'*A'lavan*. But why the chief dialect,

'or

'or mother-tongue, is to be called *Gui-*
'*púfcoan* rather than *Bifcayan*, I cannot
'tell. I have several reasons to suspect
'the good father of partiality in his
'division, and think, that, as he was
'himself a native of Guipúfcoa, he
'chose at his peril to give the post of
'honour to the language of his pro-
'vince. He ought however not to have
'excluded the *Bafque* from his division,
'since it is a sub-division of the *Bafcu-*
'*enze*, full as remarkable and distinct as
'the *Navarran*, or perhaps more. But
'why did he not take into his division
'the speech used in the small province
'of *A'lava?* He says himself of that
'speech, that *it participates of all the*
'*Bafcuenze dialects more or less contracted*
'*and varied,* " *participa de todos ellos,*
"*mas o menos fincopados y variados.*" If
'the *A'lavan* speech deserves this cha-
'racter, father *Laramendi* ought to have
'ranked it amongst the dialects of the
'*Bafcuenze.*

'It

'It is however of no great moment
'whether we adopt *Laramendi*'s divifion,
'or mine, or any other, as the Bifcayan
'language is perhaps not known at pre-
'fent to ten people born out of the
'triangle mentioned in the preceding
'letter. 'Tis true, that the Bifcayans,
'Navarrans, Guipufcoans, A'lavans, and
'Bafques, make ufe of their refpective
'dialects in epiftolary correfpondence:
'yet no man of parts and learning ever
'meddled with Bifcayan in profe or
'verfe, except a very few natives, if
'one can judge by the books that exift
'in this language. I have hunted after
'fuch books wherever I found that any
'could be got; but my collection, after
'all my pains, has proved fo very fmall,
'that it is fcarce worth mentioning.
'However, for the fatisfaction of literary
'curiofity, a page or two may very
'excufably be expended upon this fub-
'ject.

'The

' The moſt capital *Baſcuenze*-work is
' doubtleſs the folio *Dictionary*, compiled
' by the above-named father *Laramendi*,
' a Jeſuit. The dictionary bears the title
' of *Trilingue*, becauſe it runs in *Baſcu-*
' *enze*, *Caſtilian*, and *Latin*. As it has
' been printed only once, it is now be-
' come ſo ſcarce, that I could not find a
' copy of it any where, much to my diſ-
' appointment, as I am informed that its
' preface, though penned in a moſt turgid
' ſtrain, contains a great deal of rare
' erudition.

' Next the *Dictionary* comes the *Gram-*
' *mar*, compoſed by the ſame author,
' and oddly intitled *El impoſſible vencido*,
" *The impoſſibility conquered*." In that
' grammar the *Baſcuenze* is explained by
' the *Caſtilian*. I am told it has gone
' through ſeveral editions. I have that,
' which was printed at Salamanca, in
' 1729, and have repeatedly looked into
' it; but not yet to any purpoſe. In
' the *prologo*, or preface, it is ſaid, that

' *el Bascuenze es una lengua que congenia
' *poco con las otras,* " *the genius of the
" *Biscayan bears no great affinity to that of
" *other languages* ;" and my reader will
' easily give credit to this assertion, when
' he is told, that you say in Spanish, for
' instance, that BREAD is good *para
' aquel que lo come,* " *for him who eats it;*"
' which phrase is rendered in the Bis-
' cayan language by one word only:
' *jatenduenarentzat.* But, though this
' is only one word, says father *Lara-
' mendi,* we must consider it as a com-
' pound of several; as *jaten* stands for
' the verb *comér*; *du* for the accusative
' *lo*; *en* or *end* for the relative *que*; and
' *arentzat* for the pronoun *aquél* followed
' by the article *para.*

' How easily a language thus con-
' structed is to be learned, this only spe-
' cimen may possibly give an idea. But,
' were it ever so easy, no great profici-
' ency could be made in it by studying
' it out of the country where it is spoken,

' as,

' as, besides *Laramendi's Dictionary* and
' *Grammar*, the number of books printed
' in *Bascuenze* is, as I said, quite incon-
' siderable. Eleven small volumes of
' *Spiritual Discourses and Pious Medita-*
' *tions*, a translation of *Kempis's Imitation*
' *of Christ*; another translation of *Scupoli's*
' *Spiritual Combat*, a short *Catechism*,
' about half a dozen small *Collections of*
' *Prayers* in prose, and of *Spiritual Songs*
' in verse, are almost the only works to
' be found printed in this language. I
' leave my reader to judge whether it
' would be possible to learn it out of the
' country by means of the small portion
' of it, that is contained in so limited a
' library. But, was it even possible,
' would it be worth the while?

' I remember to have once read in an
' English *Magazine* an account of an
' Irish Priest, who, travelling through
' Biscay, could make shift with his Irish
' tongue, to understand the Biscayans
' and be understood by them. But whe-
' ther

'ther the author of that account im-
' pofed upon the public or not, let the
' reader determine by the help of the
' following tranfcription of the Lord's-
' Prayer in *Bifcayan* and *Irifh*. I divide it
' into fentences, that any body may with
' the greater eafe judge by the eye, whe-
' ther there is any affinity between the
' two tongués.

1.

Pater nofter qui es in cælis fanctificetur nomen tuum.

BISCAYAN.

Gure Aita ceruetant zarena erabil be-
bedi fainduqui zure icena.

IRISH.

Ar Nahir ata ere neave guh neavfiar
thanem.

2.

Adveniat regnum tuum.

BISCAYAN.

Ethor bedi zure errefuma.

IRISH.

[21]

IRISH.

Gudhaga de riaught

3.

Fiat voluntas tua ficut in cælo et in terra.

BISCAYAN.

Eguin bedi zure borondatea ceruam bezala lurream ere.

IRISH.

Gu nahium de heil ar dallugh marr thainter ere neave.

4.

Panem noftrum quotidianum da nobis hodiè.

BISCAYAN.

Iguzu egon gure eguneco og uia.

IRISH.

Thourdune nughe ar-naran leahule.

5.

Et dimitte nobis debita noftra.

BISCAYAN.

Eta barkhua detzagutzu gure corrac.

IRISH.
Moughune are veigha.

6.

Sicut et nos dimittimus debitoribus nostris.

BISCAYAN.
Guc gure gana zordun direnei barkhatcem deruztegun bezala.

IRISH.
Marvoughimon yare vieghuna fane.

7.

Et ne nos inducas in tentationem.

BISCAYAN.
Eta ezgaitzatzula utz tentamendutan erorcera.

IRISH.
Na leaghſhine a caghue.

8.

Sed libera nos a malo. Amen.

BISCAYAN.
Aitcitic beguira gaitzatzu gaicetic. Halabiz.

IRISH.

IRISH.

Agh cere fhen onululkt baigh marfon a hearna. Amen.

'At the end of his Grammar father
' *Laramendi* gives a few fpecimens of
' *Bifcayan Poetry*, which to him appear
' very fine things; and fuch they may be
' for what I know to the contrary; but
' his Spanifh tranflations of them, give
' but a very indifferent idea of the
' originals. I fee by the laft fyllables of
' the Bifcayan verfes, that the Bifcayan
' poets make ufe of *affonancies* as well as
' *rhymes* in their verfification. Which of
' the two have a better effect, I cannot
' determine: it is however not impro-
' bable, but that the *affonancies* were
' adopted by the Bifcayans in humble
' imitation of the Spaniards.

' Both in Bifcay and Navarre I have
' liftened to the fongs as well as the
' fpeech of the people, and thought the
' found of both dialects full as harmo-
' nious

'nious as those of Castile and Tuscany.
' Both Navarrans and Biscayans pro-
' nounce every letter very distinctly, and
' mark the cadence of each line so well,
' when they recite verses, as to render it
' sensible even to those who do not
' understand their language. Yet *Mr.*
' *John Farrel*, an elderly Irish merchant,
' who has resided in Biscay ever since he
' was a boy, and with whom I travelled
' from *Bilbao* to *San Sebastian*, told me
' that the Biscayan language is coarse
' and indelicate in its expressions, though
' clear and sonorous to the ear, whatever
' father *Laramendi* may say in praise of
' its elegance in the prefaces to his *Dic-*
' *tionary* and *Grammar:* nor does *Mr.*
' *Farrel*'s assertion clash with common
' sense, as a language not cultivated by
' numerous writers, must of necessity be
' to a certain degree unpolished and
' savage.

' As to the country, in which this
' language is spoken, it is mountainous
' through-

'throughout, as it lies in the very heart
' of the Pirenees. Several were the
' frightful hills that I mounted and de-
' fcended, both in Bifcay and Navarre.
' Some of their tops feemed to me quite
' as high as our Mount-Cenis, efpecially,
' one between *Berroéta* and *Lanz*, about
' mid-way between *Bayonne* and *Pam-*
' *peluna*. On the fummit of it, which
' is quite flat the fpace of about a mile,
' a wind, impregnated with frozen par-
' ticles of fnow, blew fo furioufly, that
' I thought it would throw me and my
' mule down at every ftep. But it was
' then the middle of December, and no
' wonder if it blew hard. Yet a hill
' ftill worfe was that called *La Peña*
' *Vieja, (the old mountain)* near the town
' of *Orduña*. I defcended that *Peña*
' during the night, and in February,
' along a broken zig-zag path covered
' with fnow. The path ran along the
' edges of fuch fteep precipices during
' the firft league, that would have made

' the

' the hair of many ſtand an end. Yet
' truſting to the mule, and never touch-
' ing the bridle, I came down ſafe. The
' mules are very careful how they go;
' and will ſtop, and prick their ears,
' and look how the ground lies in all
' dangerous paſſes; nor will they ad-
' vance a ſtep without being ſure of the
' next. They march with ſafety, even
' in the night. Nature has given them
' ſuch good eyes, as can guide them in
' the thickeſt darkneſs; and of this I
' have been myſelf a witneſs many a
' time, not only in the Pirenees, but
' alſo in the Alps and Apennines.

' However, notwithſtanding their high
' and frightful tops, few parts of Spain
' (and I might ſay of Europe) are ſo
' well inhabited as Biſcay and Navarre,
' proportion of ground conſidered. You
' ſee in both provinces houſes and cots
' thick-ſcattered round the higheſt places,
' and in many vallies the villages and
' hamlets are within ſight of each
            ' other.

' other. I counted above forty along
' the small river called *Orduña* from the
' town of that name; which town, as
' I said, lies at the foot of the frightful
' *Peña Vieja*. The river *Orduña* is
' formed by many springs, which issue
' out of the *Peña*, and other neighbour-
' ing hills, and runs along a valley,
' which reaches from the town of *Or-*
' *duña* to that of *Bilbao*, forming so
' many cascades between those two
' places (only six leagues distant from
' each other) that it is not navigable for
' any boats great or small.

' Although the road along that river
' proved very bad in many places, yet I
' never went an equal length of ground
' with more pleasure. Every step of-
' fered a new landscape of inexpressible
' beauty, and the frequent tumblings of
' that water delighted the sight. Both
' banks of the river seem the seat of
' fertility, and are in a manner covered
' with habitations. The people there
' have

'have taken advantage of thofe many
'cafcades, and even formed feveral arti-
'ficial ones with ftrong dikes acrofs the
'ftream. By the fide of every cafcade
'they have erected engines, by which
'they carry on various manufactures,
'efpecially that of iron, as feveral of
'the neighbouring hills yield it in the
'greateft abundance.

'Many of thofe hills produce a light
'fort of wine, which is the moft palat-
'able that ever I drank any where, par-
'ticularly that of *Orduña*, and ftill more
'that of *Serráos*, an inconfiderable vil-
'lage by the fea-fide, about mid-way
'between *Bilbao* and *San Sebaftián*. The
'natives call that wine *Chacolín*, to dif-
'tinguifh it from their other kinds of
'wine. I wonder as it lies fo convenient
'for tranfportation, that it is not car-
'ried all away to England, where, that
'of *Serráos* in particular, would be
'liked as well as *Champaign*, of whofe
'qualities it partakes. It is pleafing in

'many

'many parts of Bifcay to fee vineyards
'and corn-fields hanging reciprocally over
'each other on the floping fides of many
'hills. As it is not practicable to make
'ufe of oxen or horfes in the cultivation
'of thofe fteep fides, the corn-fields
'there are not ploughed as in other
'countries, but the foil is turned up
'by men and women with an iron-tool
'that is formed after the manner of an
'H, the lateral bars of which are about
'two foot long, and fharp-pointed at
'the lower extremities. They grafp the
'crofling bar of the H with both hands,
'thruft it by main force into the ground
'fome inches deep; then pull it down-
'wards towards themfelves by the upper
'extremities; and thus is the furface of
'every field broken and turned up.

'You may well imagine, that this
'manner of cultivation is very laborious.
'I have feen numbers of men and women
'at this work. They place themfelves
'many together in a row, each with his

'tool

'tool in hand. They all thruft at once
' the tool into the ground, all pulled at
' once, and all gradually advanced to the
' oppofite fide of the field. When the
' foil is thus turned up, they break the
' clods with iron-fpades, and form the
' furrows, which in due time are to
' reward their diligence and labour.

' As to their vines, they are neither
' bigger, nor higher, than thofe of Bur-
' gundy and the upper Monferrat. I
' mean that they are fcarcely three foot
' high, and each is tied with twigs to a
' ftake fixed in the ground.

' Befides wheat and grapes, the Bif-
' cayans and Navarrans have alfo many
' fields fowed with what in Italy is
' called *Lino*; that is, a fhort kind of
' flax, which yields very delicate fila-
' ments. They have likewife much Tur-
' key-corn, of which they make bread.
' Fruit, legumes, and pot-herbs, they
' have every where in the greateft plenty.
' The higheft and wildeft parts abound

' in

'in chefnuts of the very beft fort. Oxen
' throughout both provinces, are neither
' common, nor of a large fize; but they
' have innumerable goats, and make
' cheefe and butter of their milk. Sheep
' I did not fee many, but abundance of
' fwine in many parts; and pork is there
' as good as any where in Italy, the
' fwine being fed with fweet acorns and
' chefnuts.

' Fuel is plentiful throughout the coun-
' try, as the upper parts of the hills are
' immenfely woody. Every body may
' go and cut what fuel he needs; but that
' it may never grow fcarce, they have a
' cuftom of going once a year on a ftated
' day, the houfe-keepers and grown men
' all together, up into the woods they
' have cut, and there each man plants
' two young trees which he has taken
' with him from the nurfery in his own
' garden. When the trees are all thus
' planted, they dance merrily round a
' large *pellejo* or *leather-bag* full of wine;

' then

'then drink it, and return back to their
'homes. The inftitutor of that kind of
'feaft has certainly been a great bene-
'factor to his country.

'The fea renders fifh pretty plentiful
'fome leagues within land; and at *Bilbao*
'they have a kind called *Angullas*, which
'in my opinion is the niceft dainty pro-
'duced by the ocean. This fifh is as
'white as milk, and fo very fmall, that
'you may put two or three dozen at once
'into your mouth. The Bifcayans fry it
'in oil, and fqueeze a lemon over. It
'is fo plenty, as to be within the pur-
'chafe of the pooreft man. Boats are
'eafily filled with *Angullas* by the fifher-
'men all along the river *Orduña* below
'Bilbao down to the fea, which is four
'or five miles diftant. During that
'fpace, the river has no cafcades; fo
'that there it is navigable, and admits
'of merchant-fhips up to the fine bridge,
'that joins Bilbao with its fuburb.

'That

'That I might get some information about the Biscayan language, I staid three or four days in the town of Or-duña, as I was coming from Old Castile towards France. From Orduña I came along the river-side the space of five leagues, and rode the sixth to *Bilbao*, over some hills very high, but verdant and woody. No towns that ever I saw, are more pleasantly situated than those two. Such fertile sides of hills by them both! Such a valley! Such a pretty stream as that river! And such a soft climate even in the height of winter! I shall never see the like again!

'*Bilbao* is a very well built town, that contains above twenty thousand inhabitants. Many churches there, are of free-stone, as well as many houses. The townsmen have more public walks than they need, all bordered with high trees. But the town of *Orduña* has nothing very remarkable, except its
'romantic

'romantic fituation, though it has the
' honour, as I faid, of being the capital
' of the province. I faw but few houfes
' there with glafs-panes to their win-
' dows, whereas at Bilbao every houfe
' has that convenience. The cuftom
' of not having glafs-panes to the win-
' dows, but only fhutters, renders a
' journey through many parts of the
' Spanifh kingdom very difagreeable to a
' poor traveller, moft efpecially in winter,
' as the wind will enter at night through
' the chinks and holes of the fhutters
' into his bed-room, and render his reft
' moft uncomfortable, as has often been
' my cafe.

' Add to this inconvenience, that of
' having in numberlefs *ventas* and *pofadas*
' only one fire-place, fituated in the
' middle of what they call the kitchen;
' which is generally a large room without
' windows, with a cleft or hole at top,
' through which a dim light comes in,
' and the fmoke goes out, after it has

' almoft

'almoſt blinded you, and added to the
'blackneſs of the walls.

'In thoſe dark kitchens, and round
'thoſe fire-places, every traveller, who
'does not chuſe to ſtarve with cold, muſt
'ſit in winter on a wooden-bench or
'three-legged ſtool, though he was a
'prince, in company with the poſadero
'and his family, with every muleteer,
'peaſant, beggar, or any other perſon
'that happens to be at the poſada, while
'the maids are boiling the * *Pochéro,*
'and frying the *Abadejo.* Squeamiſh
'people would be apt to think it a great
'hardſhip to be forced to ſit in ſuch a
'dirty circle; but as for me I always
'found it the beſt part of the day, as by
'that means I had better opportunities
'than I would otherwiſe have had, of
'enjoying diſcourſes and characters not

* Pochéro *is a meſs of chick-peas and French-beans boiled in oil with onions or garlick, and* Abadejo *is ſtock-fiſh fried in oil.*

D 2 'to

' to be enjoyed out of thofe affemblies.
' I clapped the faces of the little boys,
' kiffed the little girls, fhook hands with
' the maidens, called every old man fa-
' ther, and every old woman mother;
' afked every body his name, gave fnuff
' to all, and made all drink out of my
' *borracho.* Thus I generally put them
' all in good humour, together with my-
' felf; which procured me the beft place
' by the fire-fide, and whatever little
' conveniencies the people could afford;
' nor is it poffible to go a journey
' through the kingdom of Spain with any
' fort of fatisfaction, without ufing fuch
' arts, and without fetting every body to
' chat, fing, or dance as foon as you
' alight at any place.

' I muft not omit to fay, that the Bif-
' cayans and Guipufcoans pay no fort of
' taxes. The feignory, or lordfhip,
' which comprehends both Guipufcoa
' and Bifcay, makes only a voluntary gift
' to the king of Spain when preffed by
' a war.

'a war. Few are the nations in Europe,
'that can boast of such a privilege. One
'would think, that life must be passed
'very agreeably in a part of the world
'made very beautiful by nature, as all
'Biscay is, and where people are not per-
'petually plagued with new ordinances,
'new edicts, new laws, new nonsense
'every day. We read in history, that
'the French have several times invaded
'that lordship, seigniory, or principality,
'(call it as you will) and attempted to
'make themselves masters of it; but
'were always bravely repulsed by the
'inhabitants without any great assistance
'from Spanish armies: and no wonder
'if they will fight hard in defence of
'their mountains and vallies, where they
'enjoy such a felicity, as that of never
'seeing the odious face of a tax-gatherer.
'Let us now end the *Digression*, and re-
'turn to *Fraga*.'

The Canon and I were going to sit down to supper, when Batiste rushed

haftily

haſtily in, to tell me, that *Signor Cornacchini* was juſt alighted from his chaiſe, and was coming up ſtairs. I ſuppoſe you know *Cornacchini*, as he has ſung many ſeaſons at Turin. I ſaw him once in London, whither he had been called to ſing at the opera. We ſcarcely knew each other's face; yet one is always glad to meet with people in remote places, of whom one knows ſomething. I ſent Batiſte to deſire his company to ſupper. He ſtared to hear that I was there, as my name was not quite unknown to him. Our ſlight knowledge of each other we preſently improved into familiarity. He has lived theſe laſt ſix years at Madrid, and is now going back home, loaded with the dubloons got in that capital. We have already agreed to go as far as Genoa together. At Genoa we ſhall part: he for Milan, and I for Turin. Though an Eunuch, he ſeems not to want ſenſe. I queſtion not, but we ſhall do very well together in the ſame vehicle

from

from Barcelona to Genoa. I hope he will forget the high price that gentle ladies have hitherto set upon his pretty voice, and that he will warble away for nothing during the journey. As he speaks Spanish quite fluently, and looks soft and respectful, my Canon gave no sign of that antipathy, which prevails much in this country against *los castrones Italianos,* " *the Italian goats,*" as they term such personages; so that our supper proved very chearful.

While we were at it, two Capuchin Friars came in to beg our charity. " What, said I, can I give you my good " fathers? You do not touch money, " and I am not at home to order you " some bread, or wine, or any thing " else."

'Tis true, answered the most aged of the two, that we do not touch money: but if you will give any, the *posadero* shall receive it for us.

" This is an expedient, said I, that,
" I own, I had never thought on. But
" how can you reconcile it with the
" chief rule of your inftitute? Did not
" the bleffed St. Francis order you never
" to receive money?"

The bleffed faint, replied the father, did order us not to touch it; and that we never do: but he has not forbid us to have others to receive it for us.

" You have more wit, said I, than
" our Capuchins of Italy, who never
" were able to make fuch diftinctions.
" Our Capuchins neither touch money
" themfelves, nor delegate others to re-
" ceive it. But will you give me leave,
" reverend father, to tell you, that the
" conftruction you put on St. Francis'
" order, looks no better than a quibble?
" If you are to be allowed the liberty of
" having money touched by others for
" your own ufe, the faint's command
" was childifh and ridiculous. Did he
" think it a fin to finger a piece of
" money?

" money? If he thought so, he was
" certainly wrong, since Christ himself
" touched Cæsar's coin. Then, what
" difference could St. Francis make be-
" tween touching a piece of metal, a
" piece of wood, a piece of any thing?
" However, the saint cannot be sup-
" posed to have been so simple and
" absurd, as to fancy that the mere
" touching of any inanimated matter
" was sinful; therefore when he so-
" lemnly forbade you to touch money,
" he could mean nothing else, but that
" you should abstain from the use of it,
" that you might be *the poor of Christ*
" in the strictest sense of the word. But
" that you conform to the saint's
" mandates, your desiring me to give
" money for you to the *posadero*, is no
" very great proof."

Necessity has no law, answered the Friar, without losing his temper. If our Spaniards would give Capuchins all that they want, as I suppose the Italians do,

we

we should probably do as the Capuchins of Italy. But as we do not receive from our people enough to keep us from starving, we must not only beg of every stranger that goes by, but even send many members of our community to beg in foreign provinces. But, sir, added he smiling, I only came here to ask your alms in obedience to my superior's commands, and not to debate about St. Francis' injunctions. My superior forbids me to dispute with any body that wears not a religious coat; and so you will give me leave to decline entering into controversy.

" But has your superior, said I, for-
" bidden you, to drink?"

He only orders us to be temperate, said the Friar; and if you give us leave, we will *hazer ustedes a brindis (drink your good healths)* and go about our business, as it is already too late for us to be out of our convent.

LETTER LXXI.

Don Diego again. An Irish officer. Acceptable news. Irish regiments. A fine country. An odd picture. Singing and dancing.

Mollerúsa, Oct. 25, 1760.

TO-DAY we made a push, and travelled little less than ten leagues; so that we have overtaken Don Diego Martinez and his family, much to our reciprocal satisfaction.

Early this morning we left Aragon behind us, and entered Catalonia, as *Fraga* is the last Aragonian town on this side of Spain, and *Alcaráz* (three leagues from *Fraga)* the first Catalonian village. We baited at *Alcaráz*, and went to dine at *Lérida*; a town much revered by antiquarians, who say that it was once one of the most important places in the Roman empire. At present it is but small and ill-built; considerable only for

its

its fortifications, and for a citadel feated on an eminence, which was befieged in vain during the long and bloody war, which gave the kingdom of Spain to a French prince.

The garrifon kept at Lerida feems very numerous. Being ftopped at the gate I entered, and being defired to give an account of myfelf, according to the ordinary cuftom in fortified places, I was pleafed to find that the officer, who put to me the ufual queftions, was an Irifh-man. I gueffed him to be fuch by his pronunciation, and anfwered him in Englifh, much to his furprize. From him I heard, that the Englifh have made themfelves mafters of all *Canada* in North-America. Thefe will prove interefting news to many, and I hope, when I go back to England, to find the price of beaver-hats much lowered. 'Tis one of the advantages I expect from the Englifh conqueft. The French have really managed the prefent war in a miferable

ferable manner, confidering the vaſt forces they can raiſe. But they have had their period of ſuccefs, and been a ſufficient while the firſt people in Europe. I am glad to hear that they leave room for another nation to come in; that at laſt the wheel begins moving, and going round again with ſome degree of ſwiftneſs.

The Iriſh officer, who queſtioned me at the above gate, belongs to one of the three Iriſh regiments the king of Spain keeps in his ſervice. But though thoſe three regiments are called Iriſh, they are not compoſed of Iriſhmen alone. Any man of any nation, except a Spaniard, is admitted in them as a ſoldier, and only the officers muſt be natives of Ireland or Great Britain.

At Lerida we made but a ſhort ſtay, that we might reach this place to-night; ſo that, I had not time to give a look at ſome decayed Roman antiquities there and in its neighbourhood. The ſpace we
croſſed

crossed from *Alcaráz* to this *Mollerúsa*, is inconceivably fine. There are rivulets and canals that moisten the land in different directions, and you see all along, either well cultivated fields or extensive vineyards, with olive, mulberry, plum, almond-trees in numberless orchards that have no enclosures of any kind. The pomegranates of this country are famous over Spain as well as the figs; and I am assured, that the more we shall advance towards Barcelona, the better we shall find the country.

Don Diego and his lady, a most musical pair, were much pleased to see their old acquaintance *Cornacchini*, and would have us all sit down with them to supper. When that was over, *Cornacchini* snatched a guittar out of the hands of a fellow who stood by, and sung to it a Spanish *Tunadilla* with incomparable suavity. His playing and singing brought presently a group of figures about him, not to be represented in one picture but by
the

the joint powers of *Titian* and *Calotte*. Let me sketch that picture to you with the pen, since I cannot with a pencil. The middle of it is taken up by *Cornacchini* in a languishing posture, as the words of the *Tunadilla* require. On his right there is the Corregidor and his lady, with your brother, who has Pepina in his lap. On the left there is my fat Canon, with two Augustine-Friars who are not lean, and another ecclesiastick. Then all about you see Pepina's nurse, the Corregidor's servants, my sturdy Batiste, the Canon's clown, the Posadero with his wife and children, half a dozen Calesseros with their shoes made of rope, and one half of the inhabitants of Mollerusa, some in rags, some barefooted, all silent, all looking at *Cornacchini,* and all hanging on his lips, just as the Carthaginians did on those of Eneas when he was rehearsing his dismal tale to the widow of Sicheus. But can you be so stupid, as not to guess that a most violent dancing followed *Cornacchini*'s *chini*'s finging? Upon my word, we made a merry night of it, and did not break company till one in the morning, though it had been refolved at fupper, that we fhould all fet out together at four; that is, within two hours, as I fee by my watch, it is now two. I will go and throw myfelf upon a bed without un-dreffing, that I may be ready at the calef-fero's call.

LETTER LXXII.

Too many fleas. Fare you well, Señor Don Diego. *Vifit paid to an univerfity. Manners and drefs of the ftudents in it. A fine road, and a good Venta. No broken pate.*

Venta del Violiño, Oct. 26, 1766.

AS I told you laft night, I threw myfelf on a bed as foon as I had done fcribbling, but the fleas of *Mollerúfa* are of fo fierce a kind, and have fuch formidable powers of penetration, that I could not ftand them a quarter of an hour.

This

This is one of the greatest inconveniencies that men must inevitably suffer, who travel in Spain, where there is scarce one bed in ten (I mean at the *Ventas* and *Posadas*) that is quite free from those tormenting vermin. The people of the house were still up in the kitchen, and to them I went, and chatter'd away the short time I was to stay there. As none of my fellow-travellers had undress'd, they were all ready for their chocolate against four; and at four exactly we all got into our voitures. Don Diego's trotting mules were soon out of sight. About ten we reached *Cervera*, having gone at the rate of a league an hour, and without stopping at any of the villages we met within that space. At *Cervera* I dined hastily, then ran to Don Diego's house, to take my leave of him and his good lady. I found them at dinner with some of the principal gentlemen of Cervéra. After an hour's conversation, I made my bow, and left them, not without some concern, on my side at least. Travellers ought never to familiarize themselves much with amiable people, if they would spare themselves many disagreeable sensations. But then, what pleasure would there be in travelling? The fact is, that, whether we stay at home, or go abroad, there is no pleasure of any kind, that soon or late is not followed by some pain.

As I was going to Don Diego along a fine street, I saw a considerable stone-building, and asked of a shop-keeper what it was. *The university*, answer'd the man. I must, thought I, give a look at it on my coming back; and so I did, though not at all to my satisfaction, because, as I enter'd at the gate, my ears were horribly saluted by a most infernal hissing of two or three hundred young men, who were walking under the high porticos that surround its ample court-yard.

What can this be? said I, stopping short on the upper step. The hissing mixed with cries encreased in a moment at a
dreadful

dreadful rate. In short, the meaning of it was, that the gentlemen never suffer any body to enter their university without a previous leave begg'd by a message to some of them. I had taken off my hat as I enter'd, but that it seems, will not do with their *Senorias*. I cannot say how I looked on the sudden hearing of such an uproar. They made me start back and take to my heels, not only with their hisses and cries, but, what was more efficacious, with stones that some of their most vigorous hands flung at my head. It was lucky I was not hit, and I wonder how I escaped unhurt. I was soon out of harm's way, as none attempted to follow me in the street.

Such is the reception I met at the noble university of Cervera, the glorious seat of the Catalonian muses. A fine specimen of the studies pursued there by the Catalonian youth at the expence of their king, who, as I am told, pays yearly some thousand doubloons in salaries to their instructors. Yet, in my humble opinion, his majefty would do better to fend both the ftudents and profeffors to tug at the oar in the gallies at Barcelona. The galley-mafters' whips might poffibly teach them fooner the theory and practice of that humanity, which ought to be the chief characteriftick of fcholars, and without which ftudies are pernicious. That young ftudents fhould be fo infamoufly brutal, as they are there, it is not impoffible to conceive. Young men are apt to be thoughtlefs and whimfical, and a few bad ones will foon fpoil a large number, if they are not watch'd. But that their profeffors fuffer the exertion of fuch an infamous brutality, and have it not fuppreffed, is what would make me place them at the head of the benches in a galley. My honeft Canon blufhes patriotically at my adventure, and, I think, with very fufficient reafon.

. To this account of my vifit to that univerfity I can only add, that the ftudent's drefs dress is uniform, and confifts of an ample black cloak that reaches the ground, with a large flapped hat over their other veftments.

We left *Cervera* at three in the afternoon, and came to this *Venta del Violino* to pafs the night. The road from that town to this Venta is very fine, having been but lately made on occafion of the king going to Madrid in his way from Naples. I fhall have a better bed to night than I had at Mollerúfa, this being the beft Venta I have as yet feen in Spain. It is newly built, and very well furnifhed. I am glad that I go to bed without a broken head, which would have proved pretty inconvenient in this part of the world, as you may eafily conceive.

LETTER LXXIII.

Dante*'s journey. A famous sanctuary in Spain, the history of its origin, and its romantic situation.* Batiste*'s observations.*

Piera, Oct. 27, 1760.

MY journey from *Lisbon* to *Merida*, from *Merida* to *Fraga*, and from *Fraga* to this *Piera*, might in some measure be compared to Dante's poetical journey through *Hell, Purgatory,* and *Paradise.* The country from *Cervera* to this place is formed by an uninterrupted chain of hills and dales, the amenity of which is beyond description. Were the rest of Spain so fertile and populous as this part of Catalonia, no kingdom in the world would come up to it.

The village of *Igualada,* where we dined, is as well built as any I ever saw in Italy or England; and I might say the same of all those we left behind yesterday and to day.

There

There are at *Igualada* several paper-mills on an artificial canal, and a manufactory of woollen cloth, in which I counted about forty looms. From thence I intended to let Batiste proceed with the Canon to Barcelona, and take a trip on mule-back to the convent of *Monserrate*, which is but a few leagues out of my way; but a north-wind blew so cold and so fierce the whole morning, that it made me drop the thought, as I am not cloathed warmly enough to encounter the cold of the mountain where that convent is, and was unwilling to open my trunk for a thicker dress. Had the weather continued mild, you should have been regaled with an account of an hermitage, which, as I can gather from several eye-witnesses, might cope for its singularity with that of the *Cork-Convent* in Portugal.

There is a sanctuary at *Monserrate*, which is no less famous in Spain than that of *Loretto* in Italy. I must apprise you of the origin of that sanctuary, near in the fame terms as I had it from the Canon.

"About the middle of the ninth century, when Catalonia was governed by its own fovereigns with the title of counts, there was one of them who had an only daughter no lefs beautiful than good.

"That princefs had fcarce reached fourteen, when fhe took into her head to turn hermitefs; nor was it in the power of her father's remonftrances, her mother's tears, her lover's fighs, and the people's intreaties, to make her change fo ftrange a refolution. She gave orders for a cell to be built in the wildeft part of the mountain now called *Monferrate,* where fhe retired quite alone to lead a life of prayer and pennance, feeding upon acorns and berries, and drinking of the limpid ftream.

"On the fame mountain, and at no great diftance from the royal maiden's abode, there lived a hermit called *Gua-*

rino,

"*rino*, who, though in the prime of
" youth, had already gone through so
" many voluntary austerities and suffer-
" ings, that he was reputed to be as great
" a saint as St. Jerom, St. Hilary, or St.
" Macarius?

" The devil, as you may well think,
" did not look upon this pair with a fa-
" vourable eye. He was afraid lest their
" virtue should prove contagious, and re-
" solved to oppose its effects. To obtain
" his wicked end, he tempted *Guarino* to
" go and pay a visit to the princess, un-
" der the notion of encouraging her, and
" be encouraged himself, to persevere in
" their holy course of life. The visits by
" degrees grew more frequent than was
" necessary. The consequence of them
" was, that the devil's scheme took
" place, and the princess began to swell
" about the hips, to the immense grief
" of the poor hermit, who now saw him-
" self in the imminent danger of losing

a re-

"a reputation for sanctity, which he had
"laboured hard to acquire.

"*Abyssus abyssum invocat.* What did
"the wicked *Guarino* do, in order to
"hide his wicked sin? Alas! he cut the
"young lady's throat, and secretly buried
"her body under a heap of stones!

"The dreadful feat being atchieved,
"*Guarino* went on in his wonted course,
"and continued a while to impose him-
"self for a saint upon the few inhabitants
"of the wilderness. But his crime,
"though it escaped the notice of others,
"never could escape his own; and the
"consciousness of it tormented him so
"much and so incessantly, that, unable
"to bear it, he resolved at last, to take a
"a journey to Rome, to confess himself
"to the Pope, and sue for that absolu-
"tion which, he thought, never could
"be granted him by any body but his
"Holiness.

"The Pope's hair stood an end upon
"hearing of so horrible a crime, and told
"*Guarino*

" *Guarino*, that it was not to be expiated
" but by going back to his hermitage
" quite naked and upon four, like a
" beast; adding that he was never to at-
" tempt walking in an erect posture
" again, until he received a positive com-
" mand from heaven to do so.

" The injunction was hard; yet *Gua-*
" *rino* complied with it. He stripped
" and began his journey back to Monser-
" rate. In a little time his hair grew so
" long all about his body, that he look'd
" rather like a bear, than like a human
" creature.

" Thus did *Guarino* crawl about for
" some years, avoiding as much as he
" could the few habitations that were in
" the mountain, hiding himself in a ca-
" vern by day, and going only towards
" night in search of food.

" It happened one day, that the count
" of Catalonia, father to the murther'd
" young lady, being upon a hunting
" match, saw *Guarino* as he attempted to
" clamber

" clamber over a cliff to get at some wild
" roots. The sight of so extraordinary a
" monster made the prince approach in
" order to attack it; but finding it was
" not so wild as he had conceived at first
" sight, and that it suffered two or three
" blows in a most humble posture, he
" ordered his attendants to chain it, and
" carry it to Barcelona, where he used to
" keep it in his own apartment, feeding
" it with crusts and bones as he was at
" dinner, and often diverting himself
" and his courtiers by kicking it about,
" and making it continually play a thou-
" sand anticks.

" This kind of life proved much more
" hard and mortifying to *Guarino*, than
" that of wandering about the mountains.
" Yet he bore it with such perfect pa-
" tience and resignation, that at last it
" atoned for his crime. One day as the
" count was at his dinner, and the mon-
" ster by him, a tremendous voice re-
" sounded from on high, that said, *Rise*
" *up*

" up Guarino, rife up: thy fin is forgiven.

" The poor penitent, who had long
" wifh'd in vain for fuch a command,
" ftood prefently upon two, and turning
" his eyes up to heaven, fpoke a prayer
" of thanks with audible voice and fer-
" vent emotion.

" You may well imagine the furprize
" both of the count and his attendants
" at this unexpected adventure. Having
" thus broken his feptennial filence,
" *Guarino* related with a flood of tears
" his whole ftory to the thunder-ftruck
" fovereign, and implored a pardon
" which was eafily granted. The count
" ordered him to be wafh'd and cloathed;
" then went with him to the mountain
" in fearch of the place where his un-
" happy daughter had been murthered,
" with an intention to give her remains
" a more decent burial than they had
" had from her pitilefs lover. When lo!
" miracle upon miracle! They found the
" princefs alive juft by the place where
" fhe

" she had received the wound, which was
" still open, and the blood still stream-
" ing down her breast to the ground.

" Who will attempt to tell the mixed
" grief and joy of a father at such a sight!
" He had her taken directly to her cell,
" where a surgeon soon cured her. It is
" needless to tell, that she had repented
" time enough the sins committed with
" *Guarino*, and recommended herself so
" fervorously to the Virgin Mary at the
" time he drew his knife upon her, that
" the Virgin Mary took pity on her, and
" preserved her life in that wonderous
" manner.

" As soon as the princess was restored
" to her former health, she ordered a
" church and convent to be erected on
" the very spot where *Guarino* had treat-
" ed her so barbarously. The church she
" dedicated to her patroness, not only
" for the favour received, but also because
" a most miraculous image of her had
" been found concealed just about that
" time

" time in one of the many hollows, that
" are about the mountain.

" As to the convent, the princefs
" begg'd of her father that it fhould be
" given to the Benedictine monks, who
" have fucceffively been in poffeffion of
" it from that time to this day." And
thus ends the hiftory of the miraculous *Nueſtra Señora de Monſerrate.*

That mountain I had in fight on my left hand during this whole day. It is a long ridge, that makes the oddeſt appearance at a diſtance, ſhowing many broken hills of ſeveral fizes, fome of which muſt offer very tremendous perpendicular precipices on each of their fides. The higheſt of thoſe hills denominates the whole ridge, that divides Catalonia in two pretty equal parts. The church and convent lie towards the foot of that high hill, and from thence, up through a moſt craggy winding path, you reach the ſummit of it, vifiting in your way ſeveral little hermitages formed on the various brows of the cliffs, and finding a monk in each hermitage. By the Canon's account, the various profpects from thofe hermitages muft be no lefs awful than picturefque. People of all conditions continually go from all parts of the catholic world, but moft particularly from the feveral provinces of Spain, to vifit that fanctuary, which holds as great a treafure, they fay, as that at *Loretto*, if not a greater. The monks, who are above a hundred, ufe open hofpitality to every body that goes there, be who it will, having a large income for the purpofe, befides that the order is continually fending fome of its members not only into the neighbouring provinces, but even into the moft diftant parts of the kingdom, in queft of alms for the fanctuary. It is however cuftomary for the rich that vifit it, to make fome return in money to the monks for their entertainment, and the poor only are allowed to live there for nothing during three days. The whole bufinefs business in short, is managed at *Monserrate* just as it is at *Loretto*, and there are some days in the year set a part for the celebration of solemn festivals, that draw thousands of people to visit the place, whom the monks take care to furnish with sufficient victuals and accommodations during those days.

Many are the fruitful valleys that one meets between those frightful hills; and numberless springs from the rocks join not far from the convent to form a small river called *Lobregat*, the water of which is reckoned the most salubrious in Catalonia.

The territory of *Piera*, which I chose to cross a foot towards evening, is inexpressibly fine, but I will not tire you with descriptions, that would be repeated at every step. I have just had a very good supper, and I see that the bed is clean and soft; therefore I quit the pen, and undress.

A POSTCRIPT to pleafe Batifte, who tells me, that, having alighted to drink at *Fuente de la Reyna*, a village about a league from hence, he has been told, that many of the houfes there, are well fupplied with water by means of brafscocks fixed in one of the walls of the ground-floor rooms; and he affures me, that he faw himfelf one of thofe cocks at the inn where he drank. Pray, Monfieur, fays Batifte, don't fail to note this down, faying that I made the obfervation, and not you. Thus your brothers, when they come to read your letters, fhall fee that I was not an idle fervant, but help'd my mafter as much as I could.

Batifte's defire is too juft not to be complied with, and I will alfo add, that at *Valbona*, (another village about half a league off) he has filled the *Borracho* with a wine, that I think equal, if not preferable, to the beft Syracufe I ever tafted. The honeft fellow knows very well what

he

he is about, when good wine is to be had. The villages we croffed to day, were at fo fhort a diftance from each other, as by the help of fome exaggeration one might fay, that this day's journey was performed through a fingle village.

LETTER LXXIV.

Induftry and activity of the Catalonian rufticks. Their piety. A heavy poll. A fteep hill. Vines formed into fefoons. Streets narrow, but well paved.

Barcelona, Oct. 28, 1760.

THOSE who charge the Spaniards with idlenefs, ought at leaft to make an exception in favour of the Catalonian rufticks, whom I found this morning at work by moon-light in the fields, as I walked out of *Piera* by four o'clock.

How, faid I, does it happen, that thefe people are fo diligent in quitting their

their beds, and rife fo early for fuch a purpofe? Surely the fellows get up thus betimes to their labours, that they may avoid fatiguing themfelves during the burning hours of the noon.

See how travellers are quick in finding out the reafon of things! I had fcarce formed the thought, when I laughed at my ill-natured fagacity, as I recollected that the weather was then fo cold, that the mid-day hours could not prove troublefome to the hufbandmen. Let therefore the honeft fellows have the praife they fo well deferve of an activity and induftry, which is perhaps not to be matched any where.

Nor is that activity the only quality in them that merits my commendation. Their piety has likewife a juft claim to it, as I heard them loudly recite their prayers while they bufied themfelves with their lopping-knives about their vines and mulberry-trees.

I have

I have been at times an early rifer myfelf in feveral countries, moſt eſpecially when on a journey. But although the peaſantry of every country be in general very ready to get up betimes to their works, yet I never obſerved them any where to riſe ſo early, as I find them to do in the neighbourhood of *Piera*. My good Canon aſſures me, that the Aragonians do not yield much to the Catalans in this particular; yet he owns that the Catalans are the moſt active people throughout Spain, and aſſigns a good reaſon for it. The reaſon is, ſays he, that, from the age of fifteen to ſixty, the poor Catalans are obliged to pay a capitation of * forty four reals annually, beſides their quota of the taxes that are laid in common on all ſubjects. That heavy capitation, continues the Canon, was laid on the Catalans by *Philip* V, to puniſh them for their obſti-

---
* *About twelve ſhillings Engliſh money.*

nate adherence to his competitor *Charles* in the long succession-war as they call it.

See what the little get by meddling in the contests of the great! The common people of Catalonia, and the peasantry especially, had surely no need of concerning themselves about the succession, as, whoever conquered, they were still to continue under an uncontroled government. But the multitude was always foolish throughout the world, and is always made a tool to carry points that concern them but very little, or very remotely: nor will they ever be persuaded, that with respect to them, it matters but very little how and by whom they are governed. Instead of holding their peace, and playing merely the spectators, as some other Spaniards did upon that occasion; instead of leaving the two princes to fight it out as well as they could, the silly Catalans listened to the seducive voice of numerous emissaries from Austria and from England, who

who made them believe they would all be rich, all happy, all glorious, if Charles could prevail. The effect of such promises was, that the poor fellows quitted their ploughs and their looms, took up swords and firelocks, and marched bravely against Philip, declaring that they would have a German king, and not a French one.

But what availed their declarations and their fighting! Philip prevailed, because the Germans could do but little for Charles; and the English, who had long supported him powerfully, grew at last tired of it, and dropped him. Deserted and given up by the allies of Charles, the wretched Catalans were considered by the victor as rebels and traytors. Many of them had fallen in war; but they were now hanged, beheaded, sent to the gallies, and harassed and tormented in other various ways. Then a capitation was laid upon them, and entailed upon their posterity, who are now forced to get up long before the sun to earn it, and atone for the great folly of their forefathers. *Tuas res age* is the beft general advice that prudence can give; and if every Catalan, inftead of *Biva el Rey Don Carlos*, had faid to himfelf and to his countrymen *tuas res age*, they might have prevented the great calamities that overtook them for the want of fuch an advice.

In the neighbourhood of *Piera* there is an eminent hill, the fouthern fide of which is fo fteep, that people are obliged to lay hold of ropes fixed to ftrong poles, in order to keep themfelves upright while they ftalk from vine to vine to pluck the grapes that cover all that fide. Should they truft themfelves there without the help of thofe ropes, the leaft remiffnefs of attention in ftepping, might caufe a very mifchievous tumble. I wonder how people could take it into their heads to plant vines on fo inconvenient a fpot: but the trouble of the

vintagers

vintagers is very well repaid by the goodnefs of thofe grapes, which yield the moft excellent wine that is drank in Catalonia.

About noon we reached a little village called *Molin de Reys,* where *Don Miguel de Vallejo,* brother to my friend the Canon, was waiting for his arrival, having been previoufly informed that the Canon would be there againft dinner-time.

Don Miguel had come thither in a coach and four, and had brought two more gentlemen with him. In an inftant we became the beft friends in the world, and dined chearfully together. After dinner they trotted off, after having got a promife that *Cornacchini* and I, fhall dine with them to-morrow. I walked leifurely the beft part from *Molin de Reys* to this town, with a profpect fufficiently fine all around me, to put any body in mind of the Elyfian fields. It confifted of an endlefs continuation of vines

vines fupported by mulberry-trees regularly planted, the vine-branches fo difpofed, as to form rich feftoons from one tree to the other. I have feen fuch feftooned vineyards in fome parts of Italy, efpecially in the dutchies of Mantua and Modena, with this only difference from the Catalonian fafhion, that, inftead of mulberry-trees, the Modenefe and Mantuan vines are fupported by elms.

Think how rich the Catalonian foil muft be, that affords nourifhment not only to thofe vines and mulberries, but alfo to the wheat that is fowed under their fhade! Nay, there are vineyards in this country, in which, after the corn-crop, they get another of fome other grain. What a delightful object to the eyes of the honeft hufbandman to fee fo much fertility come thus forth to reward his well-fpent labours!

During a good mile from the town the road lies perfectly even and ftraight, and is bordered on each fide by orange and mulberry

mulberry trees alternately planted. Their product, I am told, makes a part of the governor's income.

Barcelona is not three full miles in circumference, has a ſtrong fortification all ·round, and a fine citadel adjoining. The ſtreets, all paved with flat ſtones, are ſo narrow for the greateſt part, as not to admit of two voitures a-breaſt. However, thoſe who keep coaches and chariots are ſo very few, that no narrow ſtreet is embarraſſed by their concourſe. I intend to ſtay here a couple of days; but have no hopes of telling you any thing intereſting during the interval, as I do not underſtand the language of this people.

LETTER LXXV.

Situation, climate, and price of things at Barcelona. Its harbour, square, and citadel.

Barcelona, Oct. 29, 1760.

THIS is the beſt built town I have as yet ſeen in Spain, and more than ſufficiently decorated with palaces, churches, and other edifices, ſome of which would be conſidered as magnificent even in cities of the greateſt name.

The ſituation of Barcelona cannot be more advantageous, having the ſea before, a fine hill on one ſide, and a plain behind moiſtened by a number of little ſtreams, which are eaſily made ſubſervient to the purpoſes of agriculture and manufactures.

No climate is pleaſanter or healthier than this, ſays the Britiſh conſul, who has reſided here a good number of years. Frequent breezes ventilate the air in ſummer,

mer, and the little snow that falls in winter, seldom keeps a whole night unmelted on the ground. I leave you to imagine, adds the conful, how delicious the spring and autumn must be where the summer and winter prove thus temperate and agreeable.

The surprizing fertility of the country around, supplies these inhabitants with the greatest plenty of provisions; and although money circulates pretty freely amongst them by means of their commerce and manufactures, yet all the necessaries of life are as cheap here as in any of the most inland towns. Three pounds of good bread cost no more than a reál, as does the quantity of wine that would fill two bottles. Butcher's meat sells for less than half a reál the pound of sixteen ounces; and a dozen of pigeons, or a couple of the best fowl, or a full grown turkey, may be had for little more than three reals. Oil, which is an article of great consumption here, as it is in all other

other popiſh countries, ſells alſo near as cheap as wine; and pulſe, herbages, and fruit, together with ſea-fiſh of various kinds, abound at ſuch a rate the whole year round, that none needs to fear ſtarving who can but earn one reál within the four and twenty hours. Fuel ſeems to be the only thing that is not cheap in proportion to the reſt: but little of it is wanting where the mildneſs of the climate requires almoſt no domeſtick firing out of the kitchen.

The harbour of this town, though ſufficiently large, is not deep enough to receive any war-ſhips; and the ſhallowneſs of its water is cauſed by the great quantities of ſand continually driven in by the ſea.

'Tis true that there are engines conſtantly playing to clear off that ſand: yet all that thoſe engines can do, is to keep the baſon in ſuch a ſtate, as to admit of merchant ſhips not exceeding four or five hundred tons burthen.

The mouth of the harbour is secured by various batteries placed on the lower and fortified parts of a promontory, which lies on the right of the harbour as you go out, and has a full command both of the harbour and the town. *Mongiovick* is the name of that promontory, on the summit of which, as I am told, there are still some moulder'd remains of a light-house that was erected by the Romans.

Of the four gates that the town has, there are two on the sea-side, at one of which people go out, but must come in at the other. A good contrivance to facilitate the inspection of whatever is not to be introduced without the previous paying of the custom-duties.

Within the town and just by the playhouse, there is a large square called *La Rambla*, where on summer-evenings people of both sexes resort to walk and confabulate until supper-time, and often during the best part of the night, as it is the general custom in all the hot parts of
Spain,

Spain, where every town has a square, or at least a street, dedicated to such evening conversation.

The citadel already mentioned is so well kept in repair, that it looks as if it had been but lately built, though it is near two centuries old. 'Tis a large and regular hexagon, with cuvettes in the ditches, and demilunes on every curtain, besides some advanced works on the side of the country, which are all mined. It has long had the reputation of being as strong a fortress as the very strongest in Flanders: but like all citadels that are too large, and lie on a flat ground, it requires little less than an army to defend it; and you know what a dreadful inconvenience attends numerous garrisons, which are soon starved when the enemy has once possessed himself of the country around.

LET-

LETTER LXXVI.

A new town. Las Minas and Gages are two brave men.

Barcelona, Oct. 30, 1760.

Commerce has of late years been here thriving at such a rate, and causing such an exorbitant addition of inhabitants, that the government, unwilling to enlarge Barcelona at the expence of its surrounding fortifications, yet desirous to assist an encrease of population which might have been checked for want of room, order'd that a new town should be built about a mile distant from this.

What name this new town is to have, seems not yet determined. Some call it *la Ciudad Nueva*, some *Barcelona la Nueva*, and some *Barceloneta*. I suppose that its limits will depend on the concourse of builders and settlers, who will contract or enlarge the present outline, which encloses an oblong square, half a mile on
one

one fide, and three quarters of a mile on the other.

It gives pleaſure to ſee the pretty uniformity of what is already built, as the parts of every houſe run parallel from end to end of every ſtreet. No houſe has more than two ſtories, beſides the ground-floor; and the ſtreets are wide enough to admit of two and even three vehicles a-breaſt. The outſide of every houſe is cover'd with white plaiſter, which, as it was laid on very ſmooth, ſhines like marble, but half poliſhed. Yet the glare proves not offenſive, becauſe the inter-columniations are coloured with a pale red, and the window-ſhutters (all outwardly placed) are painted green.

On condition that they conform to that plan of ſtrict uniformity, and provided they be Catholics, ſtrangers are admitted, indiſtinctly with the natives, to build there as many houſes as they chuſe; and, as well as the natives, they have

have the foil for nothing and for ever, upon which they chufe to build.

To this advantage you may add two more: that of naturalizing themfelves by fuch means, without any other formality, and of having the faith of government pledged that they fhall never pay any ground-rent, nor other tax whatever, on account of any building, whether houfe, ftorehoufe, or of any other kind that they may there erect.

The renowned Marquis *de las Minas*, who has been fome years governor of this principality, gives himfelf no reft in forwarding the building of this new town: and fuch have been his efforts, that it contains already three thoufand inhabitants, amongft whom there are not a few who are merchants and traders of confiderable note.

Befides the pecuniary affiftance that the generous marquis has afforded to fome in the building of their houfes, and the various fums lent without intereft to others,

others, in order to enable them to settle there, he has also laid out several thousands of (*a*) doubloons (not less than twenty thousand) in erecting a most magnificent church, which is to serve the new town as cathedral. Many parts of that church are of white marble, especially the front, which is not wanting in pillars, statues, and other costly ornaments. A noble fellow that *Las Minas*, and much more estimable for the lofty spirit which makes him forward that work, than for the generalship which render'd him formidable in Italy during the last war! I cannot help remarking, that the two very generals who chiefly commanded in that war against us and the Germans, happen at this present time to prove the two greatest benefactors of this country, as *Las Minas* is building a new town in Catalonia, while *Gages* is making new roads throughout Navarre.

(*a*) *A doubloon is about fifteen shillings English money.*

L E T-

LETTER LXXVII.

Knives faſtened to the tables. Various manufactures. Plenty of Taylors, and why. A coach hired.

Barcelona, Oct. 31, 1760.

THE additional tax of forty four reals, was not the only puniſhment inflicted on the Catalans for their ſiding with the competitor of Philip V. The uſe of all ſorts of weapons was interdicted them, and with ſo much rigour, that they not only were forbidden under the moſt ſevere penalties to carry a knife in their pockets, but they were not even permitted to have more than one at table; and that one they were alſo commanded to ſecure to the table itſelf by a long chain, for the uſe of carving and cutting when at their meals.

It is probable that the Catalans did not fail to ſubmit to this odd law while it was new. But as the government has had no reaſon this long while to ſuſpect them

them of difaffection, no body now cares what knives they carry in their pockets, nor how many they have on their boards. However, the cuftom ftill continues amongft the lower claffes, and at the *pofadas* and *ventas*, to have a large carving-knife faftened to an iron chain; the chain nailed to the table-corner.

Far from being difaffected to the prefent government, the Catalans feem quite enamoured of their king; and for no bad reafon, as his majefty forgave the principality every *maravedi* of the arrears that were due to the royal treafury, on the day that he landed on this fhore from Naples. Thofe arrears had gone on encreafing during three or four years when the harvefts had not proved plentiful, and amounted to little lefs than two hundred thoufand pounds fterling at his majefty's arrival. To remit fuch a fum was an act of munificence, which, as it was accompanied by many gracious words, quite won him the hearts of thefe people; and

all

all traces of paſt ſufferings and paſt reſentments ſeem now intirely obliterated.

As Cadiz is the moſt flouriſhing town the Spaniards have on the Ocean, ſo is Barcelona on the Mediterranean. Many are the manufactures that are here carried on with a ſpirit not much known in other parts of Spain; and the moſt conſiderable of them I take to be that of firelocks and piſtols, of which theſe armourers make enough to furniſh near the whole kingdom, beſides the vaſt numbers ſhipped off for the Spaniſh dominions in the new world. I am even aſſured that the Neapolitan troops are ſupplied with ſuch weapons from this town, in conſequence of the regulations made by this king before he placed his ſon upon the throne that he quitted for this.

Next to the fire-arms manufacture comes that of edged weapons, razors included, with whatever comes under the denomination of ſteel-ware. The blades of Barcelona have the reputation of being
little

little inferior to thofe of Toledo; and the razors made here, I prefer to thofe of England, now I have tried them fufficiently; though not for their beauty or finenefs, but only for their make, as they do quicker execution upon a ftrong beard, in confequence of their being broader and heavier than the Englifh razors.

The manufacture of woolen blankets is alfo one of the moft confiderable. No lefs than eighty thoufand of them are yearly exported to various nations. The Italians buy about fix thoufand a year for their fhare. This I have been told at *Don Miguel*'s by a gentleman, who has fome infpection over the trade and manufactures of this town.

It is needlefs to mention the Barcelona-handkerchiefs, as they are known throughout Italy full as well as thofe of *Vigévano*. Some of thefe handkerchiefs were fhown me, that fell for eighty, and even a hundred reals a-piece; and I own

that

that I never faw any thing finer of the kind. The beft that come from the Eaft-Indies are but indifferent when compared to the beft that are made here.

Few towns, in proportion to their extent, abound with fo many taylors as Barcelona, becaufe the greater part of the cloathing for the Spanifh troops, both in Spain and beyond fea, is made here.

At the requeft of *Don Miguel* I have been permitted to vifit the *Tarazána*; that is, the arfenal, or dock, in which they build but very few fhips, and of the inferior fizes only. But it is there that the king of Spain has his greateft foundery for great guns, and there is caft almoft all the cannon the kingdom wants, befides what is fent to America. Many are alfo the military ftores that are provided in that arfenal, both for the fea and land fervice; but the enumeration would be long and tedious.

'Tis

'Tis now near noon, and *Cornacchini* calls me to dinner that we may be gone this afternoon, and advance some leagues homewards before it is night. In partnership with an Andalusian clergyman who goes to Rome, we have hired a coach that is to carry us so far as *Antibes* for * five and twenty doubloons. Six female mules are to draw it, and two stout fellows to lead it. *Batiste* and *Cornacchini's servant* shall ride on the coach box; and considering what a quantity of luggage we carry, together with the distance between *Antibes* and *Barcelona*, I think we go very cheap. The clergyman has no servant, and but a small portmanteau; therefore we have agreed that he shall pay but a trifle. We would even have given him his passage for the mere pleasure of his company, if he had been willing to accept of it. As yet we are perfect strangers

* *Little more than eighteen pounds English money.*

to each other, as he came to us from another inn, to know whether we could make room for him in the coach. He looks rather cloudy than ferene, nor do we expect that he will prove fo agreeable as my Canon of Siguenza. However I hope, with *Cornacchini*'s affiftance, to make him prove focial and merry, whatever his looks may forebode.

I have nothing to add with regard to Barcelona, but that the *locanda*, or inn, called *la Fonda*, is by much the beft I have as yet been in fince I left London. 'Tis kept by an honeft Milanefe, who deals largely in wine, and exports quantities to feveral parts of Europe. His wine-vaults are one of the greateft curiofities in this town. He made me pay at the rate of fourteen reals a day for a good dinner, a good fupper, and a good bed. I don't think he has gained a real by the bargain.

LETTER LXXVIII.

Politeness of custom-men. Manner of travelling in Catalonia. Catalonian buskins. Names of the she-mules.

Lináz, or Linaréz, Oct. 31, *at night*, 1760.

AMONGST the benefactors of mankind I venerate none so much as him who invented the letters of the alphabet. By the easy means of about two dozen of signs, to acquaint even the unborn with whatever we see, hear, think, and do; 'tis a wonderful art! Blessed be the memory of him who found it.

In that art I have long laboured to acquire the reputation of a skilful man, and am unwilling to believe that my endeavours have proved entirely vain. But grant my powers of combining those two dozen of signs, to be ever so prodigious, yet it would not be possible to form

form a good letter with the account of what I heard, faw, thought, or did between the town of *Barcelona*, and the village of *Lindz*, as I neither faw, nor heard, nor thought, nor did any thing deferving the leaft alphabetical decoration: and I would fpare you the trouble of reading that account, were it not for that kind of obligation I am now under, to keep up to the ufual method of daily writing whenever I have a quarter of an hour to fpare.

We left Barcelona a little after one. At the gate we came out, the cuftommen relied upon our word that we had nothing cuftomable amongft our things, and civilly exempted us from the vexation of feeing our trunks difcompofed. It is faid in feveral itineraries through Spain, that travellers are infolently treated by that fort of people, to the end that they may extort what ought not to be extorted: but whatever may have been the practice of former times, I may now

now aver the contrary from my own experience at five Spanish custom-houses; that is, at Badajóz, Toledo, Madrid, Zaragozza, and Barcelona.

Our mules did not cease trotting and galopping, till at six we reached this village of *Lináz*. The country we crossed is all beautiful and thickly inhabited by poultry and swine, as well as by men. We ran little less than seven leagues in about five hours. I must tell you how our two muleteers manage this journey. One of them sits on the coachbox, not to hold any rein or bridle, which are no parts of the beasts' accoutrement, but only to lash them with a long whip, and hoot, and cry, and frighten them straight onwards, while the other does the same as he runs a-foot like a desperado. Each mule has been made acquainted with her own name by dint of blows, as I take it; and it is surprising to see how each of them is obedient to the voices of our conductors, and with what promptitude each quickens or flackens her pace, and conforms to the march of the reft the inftant fhe is bid.

Having enjoyed his feat for about a mile, or a mile and a half, the fellow jumps down; and his companion fprings up into it, with a nimblenefs that would do honour to a cat. Such is to be their alternate exercife during the journey. They both wear light jackets and thin trowfers, and have their feet adorned with the Catalonian bufkin, which is formed of a piece of leather wrapped round the foot, and tied over the ancles in a manner, that appears odd enough to an unaccuftomed eye. I fhall walk but very little through France if the fellows go every day the pace they went this afternoon; and fhall of courfe have but very little to write, as he that runs inftead of walking, cannot fee much, though he had the eyes of Argus.

Here

Here you have the names of our she-mules. *Roxa, Fea, Mohina, Parda, Chica, Rapofa.*

LETTER LXXIX.

The great mountains are in fight. An adventure which makes room for fome political confiderations.

Puentemayór, Nov. 1, 1760.

FOR the firſt time in my life I was to-day admitted into the noble prefence of the Pirenean mountains, an honour I had longed for thefe many years, as I often heard that their eminencies were the only rivals their highneffes the Alps ever had in Europe.

The nearer I have been approaching thofe tremendous hills ever fince I croffed the river *Cinca*, the more I have found the people courteous and refpectful. Almoſt every man I look at, pulls off his hat, and every ſhe drops me a curtefy.

curtefy. No muleteer, no pedlar, no ruftick do I fee at his victuals in the inns I enter, but will point ferene to the difh before him, and beg of me to partake of his meal if he catches my eye ftopping but an inftant upon what he is eating, or when I exprefs the ufual wifh, that much good may it do him.

Having dined at a place called *Las Mallorquinas*, we croffed *Girona* towards evening, and came to this village of *Pontemayór* to fleep.

Girona is a large and fortified town, that feems full of people. It has fome fine public walks out of the gates, and a territory that appears delightful. This is all I can tell you of *Girona*, as we did only crofs it without alighting: but we met with a fmall adventure there, that I judge to be well worth recording.

As we entered at the gate, an officer of the garrifon who kept guard there, bid us with a pretty infolent tone of voice to produce our paffports, putting on a moſt ill-humoured frown while he aſked us the cuſtomary queſtions about our reſpective qualities, and affecting to ſtare us in the face with a look of contempt that every one of us thought to be tolerably odious.

Strange, that any body ſhould be ſo wrong-headed, as to make himſelf diſagreeable without a ſhadow of provocation, and prove offenſive to no manner of purpoſe! Yet there are mortals in this world, who will behave with ſuch unaccountable groſſneſs for no other apparent reaſon, but to have you informed, that they are worthleſs and hateful brutes, and dare to ſhow that they are ſuch.

Mine officer was the ſecond ſhocking Spaniard I have as yet met in Spain. Do you remember the old Colonel at * *San Pedro?* That Colonel was the firſt. However the moſt beaſtly of the two was undoubtedly the officer, who, be-

* See letter XLII.

ſides

fides his abfurd rudenefs to us, took the liberty to give a kick to one of our muleteers, and for no other reafon but becaufe he betrayed fome impatience at our being detained there longer than the reading of our paffports required while night was approaching, and we had ftill two leagues to go.

The infolence of that officer, confidered together with that of the old Colonel at *San Pedro*, makes me think, that much military overbearing takes place in this country, as it does in many other: in our dear Piedmont, for inftance, where the formidable fons of Mars often affume the privilege of being infolent to the lower claffes, and treating them arbitrarily with total impunity.

What a difference between thofe countries and the glorious ifle of Great Britain, where neither Colonel nor Captain, nor indeed any perfon of any rank whatfoever, dares to treat the meaneft plebeian with fuch indignity as that of the *Girona-*

officer to our muleteer, or the *San Pedro-*Colonel to our caleſſeros!

So far, you will ſay, the Engliſh are much better off, than the Spaniards and the Piedmonteſe; and ſo far the conſtitution of their government ought to be that of every government. But every medal has its reverſe, as we phraſe it; and by way of counterballance to that advantage, the Engliſh labour under a diſadvantage, to which a Spaniard and a Piedmonteſe could no more be reconciled, than an Engliſhman to the arbitrary behaviour of a Spaniſh officer to a Spaniſh muleteer.

The diſadvantage I mean, is, that the lower claſſes in England make by much too light of the higher, and ſeem to have no reverence for what in all countries is conſidered and termed the better ſort. The Engliſh populace will too often force even a lord to give a ſilly cry in favour of this and that candidate at an election, and tumble a gentleman into the mud,

or

or fling dirt at his coach, or break his windows, upon their coming to the knowledge that such a gentleman is not of the party, which mere chance, or fondness for noise, or some such other potent cause, has made them espouse the day or the week before. The English populace will stop the vehicle of a lady going to a mask, and force her with a most arbitrary violence to uncover her face, that they may look at her: a piece of rudeness that nothing could reconcile mankind to, but the fondest partiality to national abuses and irregularities when grown inveterate. What signifies enumerating instances of the contemptuous irreverence, with which the high in England are treated by the low? Too many might be produced, that would make a Spaniard shudder as much as I did at the brutal conduct of the officer of today.

Such is the natural perverseness of human nature, that it will never be possible for human wifdom to ftrike out a fet of laws, fufficient to contain both the great and the fmall within juft limits, and keep government equidiftant from the rocks of tyranny and the fhallows of licentioufnefs. Truft the better fort with any portion of arbitrary power, and you render them haughty and oppreffive: but on the other hand, what will be the confequence if you fhorten the diftance between the great and the fmall by means of laws of a levelling tendency, and thus attempt to allay the natural bitternefs of the life that the poor multitude muft lead? That fame poor multitude will foon turn daring in this cafe; will prove untoward and difrefpectful; and will even be tyrannical on many and many occafions. Which of the two evils will you decide to be the lighter? The infolence of the great to the fmall, or that of the fmall to the great?

Baftiáno, faid I to the Muleteer while we were at fupper, I muft give you thanks

thanks for your prudence in putting up with the brutality of the Captain at *Girona*. Had you refented it, who knows how the foldiers upon guard would have treated us all, and how long they would have detained us there!

For my part, interrupted Batifte with fury, had the officer ufed me as he has *Baftiáno*, I would have given him *un coup de piftolet*.

Hablas como loco, quoth Baftiano.

Batifte, faid I, your friend Baftiano fays, that *you talk like a fool*. But pray, *Monfieur le Bravache*, what piftol would you have made ufe of to kill the officer? Have you forgotten, that at *Zaragozza* you loft the only one we had, fince its fellow was ftolen from us by the foldiers at *Talavera*? But look here, my friend *Baftiano*. I fay, that I approve very much of your calm conduct at *Girona*, for which *el Señor Cornacchini* and I have refolved to make you this fmall prefent. By your prudence you faved us fome trouble:

trouble: You therefore deserve some acknowledgment from us. Continue to behave like yourself to the end of our journey, avoid with the utmost care to bring yourself or us into any squabble, and we shall not forget you and your companion when at *Antibes*. Nor do you mind this silly Frenchman, who will swagger, and vapour, and cleave mountains, because he has none of your manly good sense and christian coolness.

This short exhortation, which I thought necessary at the eve of entering France, will, I hope, have a good effect on the mind of two fellows, whom I have already taken notice to be actuated by national antipathy; a thing that no traveller ought to have himself, nor suffer any of his people to show at any rate.

LETTER LXXX.

An inn burnt down. Passage through the Pireneans performed by moon-light. Arrival at Perpignan.

Fitou, Nov. 3, 1760.

YEsterday at five in the afternoon we reached *La Jonquiera*, a poor village, and the last on this side Spain. An hour after we crossed an inconsiderable river over a bridge, one half of which belongs to Spain, and the other to France. From that bridge we went up a most difficult ascent, and within another hour had an imperfect view of a fortress called *Bellegarde*, which they say is impregnable because it is unapproachable. If it is really unapproachable, it must be impregnable without doubt.

Not far from that fortress we stopped on a small flat, amidst some cliffs as high

high as the higheſt ſteeples. There our Muleteers had told us we ſhould get an excellent ſupper, and have very good beds. But, as ill luck would have it, the Inn, where theſe bleſſings waited for our arrival, had been accidentally ſet on fire about a week ago, and nearly burnt down to the ground; ſo that the good ſupper we were to have, was limited to ſome bread and cheeſe: and as for beds, we contrived one in a room without ceiling, and placed our gentle Muſician in it, as the moſt delicate perſon in company, on condition that he ſhould ſing us a ſong before he fell aſleep: then we laid ourſelves down in the ſame room, and without undreſſing, upon ſome bundles of ſtraw, which were procured from a neighbouring ſtable.

At four in the morning I awaked, and as my couch was none of the moſt inviting, I did not chooſe to give a turn on the other ſide, but got up and ſtole away to another roofleſs place, which

but

but a week ago was called the kitchen. The poor undone landlord was there with his wife and fon, making fome breakfaſt ready for the Muleteers. The lad I defired to come and ſhow me the way, as I intended walking to the next town, and there wait for my company. The moon, though much on the decline, ſhone bright enough on many fummits to afford a fufficient glimmering for me to form an idea of the alternate faſtneſſes and precipices, through which the road has been contrived, fo ample and convenient as if it had been ſtruck out in the midſt of a plain. The expence of that road muſt have been very confiderable.

It is not poſſible to expreſs my gloomy fatisfaction as I was walking along the immenfe majeſty of thofe tremendous hills; nor can I tell the vaſt, but broken thoughts, that fwarmed in my brains, furrounded as I was by the amplitude of that filence. Some fenfation of the fame

inex-

inexpreffible kind I had felt when the kingdom of England became a fpot fcarcely difcernible, and an immane undulation ftrove to drive out of my mind every image but that of water.

It was broad day when I reached the village of *Boulou,* half diftracted by a canine hunger, which I think would foon have turned into rage, if an innkeeper had not immediately affifted me with fome food. 'Tis furprifing how the powers of digeftion are quickened by the fharp air of high mountains : and with the effects of that air I have been fo long acquainted, that I was inexcufable not to put a piece of bread in my pocket.

Thus was my paffage performed acrofs the Pirenees, which, throughout their long chain, are no where fo narrow as between *la Jonquiera*'s bridge, and the village of *Boulou*; the intermediate diftance being only three leagues. How pleafed I fhould be to have it in my

power

power to walk over every part of them, as I did from the burnt inn to *Boulou*, and make myself thoroughly acquainted with their nature and productions; and, what would prove still more satisfactory, with the several speeches and modes of life of their several inhabitants! A complete account of those mountains from sea to sea, would in my opinion prove one of the most entertaining that ever was written: but *non omnia possumus omnes*, and the desires and schemes of every man, always go much beyond his powers.

Spain at last is fairly left behind, and I shall soon be so far from it, as not even to see the loftier tops of those hills, which divide it from France. But before I get at any greater distance from those enormous masses, let me speak a few words more of the Spaniards, and take myself to task for the opinion I long entertained of them before I undertook this journey.

Upon

Upon the credit of several books I had long fancied, that nothing was to be found throughout so vast a kingdom, but slothfulness and superstition, strongly connected with haughtiness and impertinence. I had read that the Spanish Grandees and higher Gentry, were so strangely educated, as to think it a shameful derogation from their quality to apply to any kind of study; therefore, that ignorance extended even so far in the greatest part of them, as perfect inability to read their own books, and that they would not even deign to know the different values of their own coins.

Amongst their people of the second or middle ranks, I had read that study was not held in total aversion, but that nine in ten of them used to wear large spectacles even within their own doors, that people might be thus cheated into a belief of their great knowledge, which was to be supposed as acquired at the expence of a good part of their sight : And
as

as to their lower claſſes I could almoſt have taken my oath, that there was not one man in a thouſand endowed with ingenuity enough to make a button; nor did I expect to find any of their ruſticks ſo far ſkilled in country-buſineſs, as to know how to dung a field, open a ditch, rear a cow, or lop a willow.

Such, or nearly ſuch, are the notions that they will form, who ſhall give implicit faith to the greater part of the books written by itinerant authors about Spain and its inhabitants. You will ſee how far I can now conform to thoſe notions, when you ſhall have read my preſent Journal, and confidered what degree of probability accompanies my accounts. I hope you will have no reaſon to ſay, that they were penn'd by prejudice, by bigotry, and by impertinence.

The coach came to *Boulou* juſt as I had done my breakfaſt, and the cuſtom-houſe-men were ready to ſearch our portmanteaus, or rather to get ſome little money

money to exempt us from their search. According to the French practice, we had leaden seals affixed to each of our portmanteaus; by which means travellers are enabled to cross all France if they chuse, without receiving any further molestation at the other customhouses, except they break off those seals.

We then trotted to the town of *Perpignan*, which is the capital of *Roussillon*, of which I can say nothing, as we did not enter it, but stopp'd to dine at an inn in the suburb. It is surrounded with fortification, and has a citadel on a neighbouring eminence, where they show a centry-box on the corner of a bastion, down which the Emperor Charles V, going once alone the nightly round, tumbled a soldier into the ditch, as he found him sleeping on his post, and stood centry himself until the guard came to relieve him.

I wanted to give a look to the Cathedral of Perpignan, which I am told is

one

one of the largeſt Gothick buildings they have in France, but had not time.

During the afternoon we travelled along the fineſt road that ever was cut through any country, and reached this *Fitou* as the fun was going down. The Speech uſed in *Rouſſillon* is as hard to underſtand as the Catalonian, and at the inn at Perpignan there was not a foul that could ſpeak either French or Spaniſh.

LETTER LXXXI.

A new method adopted. Light mention made of ſeveral places.

Beziers, Nov. 4, 1760.

THOUGH I am ſtill nine or ten hundred miles from home; yet the daily accounts of my journey you muſt conſider at an end, as we do not ſtop any where long enough for me to caſt my eyes about, and make inquiries. France more-

moreover has been vifited by fo many travellers, and every part of it fo often and fo minutely defcribed, that it would be very difficult for me to difcover new fubjects for obfervation, and make new additions to what may be found in books, if I had even leifure to infpect and to examine, efpecially as I am quite ignorant of the fpeeches both of Rouffillon and Languedoc.

I intend therefore to forbear for feveral nights my cuftomary fcribbling, and continue idle until I meet with any thing that I may conceive to be worth a letter. However I fhall fet down the names of the places we fhall progreffively fee, and even make fome flight remark upon fome of them, juft as it fhall happen, rather by way of memorandum to myfelf, than with the ufual view of conveying any fort of information to you. Here is the firft fpecimen of the new method I intend to follow in the profecution of my itinerary.

Nov.

Nov. 4. We dined at *Narbonne*, and supped at *Beziers.*

Narbonne, a considerable town, is parted in two by an artificial Canal, that was cut out of the river *Aude.* The canal bears Boats that can carry thirty and even forty tuns. By means of those Boats the inhabitants of Narbonne can drive some trade, as their Canal communicates both with the sea, and with the renowned great *Canal* of *Languedoc.*

The curiosities at Narbonne are, the Cathedral, the Archbishop's palace, a College termed *the Seminary,* and I know not what else. But what I thought most remarkable, were the short petticoats of the women, which scarcely reached below their knees. Our Andalusian Companion seemed quite shock'd at such a fashion. The situation of Narbonne is a disgustful bottom surrounded by hills that are reckoned pleasant and fertile.

Beziers, a small town, is seated on an eminence, from which many fine prospects

spects are commanded. I saw nothing in it any way remarkable, except a clumsy stone-statue representing a stout fellow, who, in the days of *La Pucelle* defeated alone an army of Englishmen.

Nov. 5. Dined at *Pezenás*, or at *Pezenásque*, and supped at *Gigean*. *Gigean* is nothing. *Pezenás* is a small town, as pleasantly situated as you can imagine. There is *la Grange des prés* just by the town, which they say, is the finest house in Languedoc, and belongs to a Prince of the blood who never goes to see it.

Nov. 6. Dined at *Montpellier*, and supped at *Pont de Lunél*.

Montpellier is called in Latin *Mons puellarum*, " the hill of the maidens," because it was built near an Hermitage inhabited by some holy maidens. But our modern maidens (say the wits of Montpellier) think little of holiness and much of science; and are generally so knowing, as to have little left to learn *le jour de leurs noces*.

The

The town, irregular and ugly, swarms with Apothecaries, Distillers, Chymists, and Quacks of all kinds, who fill the world with Alkermes, Mithridate, Theriac, Waters, Oils, Syrups, Essences, Pomatums, Perfumes, and other such drugs. It is said that the junior Scaliger gave the preference to Montpellier above all other towns in France, for the pleasantness of its situation, the salubrity of its air, and the sociableness of its inhabitants. I have nothing to say to the two first qualifications of Montpellier: but how could its inhabitants be considered very sociable just at a time, when Calvinism and Discord raged most among them, and caused numberless scenes of blood throughout Languedoc?

The environs of *Pont de Lunél* produce a Muscadel-wine, that has a reputation.

Nov. 7. Went by *Nimes* in the morning, saw [from the coach] a side of its

Amphitheatre, dined at *Tarafcon*, and fupped at *St. Remy*.

The inhabitants of *Tarafcon* fay, that their town is fo named from a ferpent called *Tarafca*, which was kept tame by *Sancta Martha*, Sifter to *St. Mary Magdalen*. In Spain they call *Tarafca* an imaginary great ferpent, as alfo a huge wooden giant which precedes fome of their proceffions on holy days. The town of *Tarafcón* and that of *Bouçáire* face each other, and the River Rhone runs betwixt. They are joined by a bridge.

Nov. 8. Dined at *Orgon*, and fupped at *Lambéz*, or *Lambefc*.

Both fmall towns, and both belonging to the *Count de Brionne*, a great French Lord, who lives at Paris.

Nov. 9. Dined at *La Puifiere*, and fupped at *St. Maximin*.

At *St. Maximin* a good number of holy relics is preferved in a fubterraneous Chapel of a Church dedicated to the Saint who gave his name to the town.

The

The following are the moſt capital among thoſe relics.

A Vial ſaid to be filled with the blood of our Saviour, that was gathered on mount Calvary by Mary Magdalen, and brought into this part of the world by herſelf.

Mary Magdalen's head, wanting but one tooth, which was ſtole by an Archbiſhop, and carried to Touloufe.

Both elbows of Sancta Martha, Siſter to Mary Magdalen, with whom ſhe came to live in Provence after our Saviour's death, accompanied by *St. Maximin,* who was one of the ſeventy Diſciples.

The arm-bones and ribs of the chaſte Suſanna, cum multis aliis.

Though it was quite dark when we reached *St. Maximin,* yet the Andaluſian Prieſt and I prevailed upon a Dominican Friar to ſhow us that Church. It is much larger than any we have in Turin, as far as I could judge through the darkneſs imperfectly broken by the light of a lanthorn we had with us, and of two or three lamps hanging lighted before as many altars.

Are you sure (said I to the Friar) that these relics are genuine?

Tout le monde ici (answer'd the Friar) *le croit comme un artile de foi.* " Every body " here believes it as an article of faith."

The staple-commodity of *Saint Maximin,* as at *Loretto,* are chaplets of glass-beads, which the women of the place oblige strangers to buy, whether they have a mind to it, or not. A number of those women entered my room at the inn, and forced a rosary upon me, in spight of my teeth. However, the expence was but a few *liards,* and they flatter'd me for a louis-d'or at least, to come at that little money.

Nov. 10. A most heavy rain troubled us the whole day, and overflowed the road in such a manner, that we had been in danger if we had not hired several peasants to support the coach, and

keep

keep it upright in several places. We had a bad dinner at *Bagnoles,* and a worse supper at *Luc.*

LETTER LXXXII.

A spot once favoured by Cesar. An Andalusian epicurean, and a learned innkeeper.

Frejus, Nov. 11, 1760.

THE rain has continued so hard ever since we left *St. Maximin,* that it kept us till twelve this morning quite shut up in that wretched inn at *Luc.* At twelve the sky turning somewhat clear, we set out and went six leagues without stopping, which brought us to this small town of *Frejus.* A great part of the road was perfectly overflown, which, as I am told, is always the case whenever it rains during a whole day, because of the many torrents that jointly descend from the neighbouring hills: so that, we were obliged again to have peasants

with

with us, some to wade through the waters and show the way to the muleteers, some to keep by our side and support the coach in case of accident. It would otherwise not have been possible to go onwards without running the danger of an overset.

Mine host of *Frejus*, who piques himself upon his literature, showed me his books while supper was making ready, and informed me, that in this town there are the remains of an amphitheatre and of an aqueduct, both built, as it is thought, by Julius Cesar, who resided here a while, and gave his name to the place, calling it *Forum Julii*, which in time degenerated into *Frejus*. Cesar, continues the learned inn-keeper, used to keep here a large fleet, as *Forum Julii* was in his days a sea-port-town, and not a poor *bourg*, as it is at present. The sea has long been withdrawing from us, and is now half a league off; so that vines and olive-trees are now growing

on

on the very spot, where *Triremes* and *Quinqueremes* used once to ride at anchor.

It was quite dark when we alighted: therefore, instead of going to give a look to those ancient remains, we set down to eat a modern supper, which *Cornacchini* and I thought quite excellent. But what we think excellent is called execrable by our Andalusian companion, who seems to have been born with an unconquerable abhorrence to turbots and pigeons. He could taste of neither, because neither the pigeons nor the turbot were seasoned with that nice salt-butter the Andalusians get in large barrels from Flanders. Poor man! He has led a most penitent life ever since we entered France, where it is impossible to have chick-peas boiled with onion, stock-fish stewed in oil with garlick, and rotten olives by way of desert. So various are the appetites of men, that what is thought a dainty by one, seems poison

to

to another. Thanks to my kind ſtar that gave me a true traveller's palate: a palate univerſal, which is afraid of nothing that can honeſtly bear the name of food. Let it be but dinner-time, and I care not a fig for the difference between macaroni and roáſt-beef, herring and frogs, the olla and the fourcrout: a very coſmopolite on the article of filling one's belly.

LETTER LXXXIII.

Remains of an aqueduƈt. Wiſdom of the Romans. The Madroño. *The iſle of* St. Marguerite. *Situation of* Antibes.

Antibes, Nov. 12, 1760.

HAVING left Frejus this morning by break of day, we ſoon ſaw on each ſide of the road a great many broken remains of the Roman aqueduƈt mentioned yeſterday by our learned antiquarian the inn-keeper. There is ſomething that looks both rural and majeſtic

in

in thofe remains, richly clad with fhrubs and weeds of different kinds, and efpecially with overgrown ivy.

That aqueduct, as it appears by its ruins, extended a great way over the country, and carried the water of fome diftant fpring or river, the traces of which are not now to be found. That was one of the moft laudable provifions of the Romans, to build a great many works of that kind throughout their vaft empire, that they might fpread fertility far and near. Thus they removed barrennefs even from the moft ftubborn defarts, nor did any land remain uncultivated wherever it could be moiftened by means of an aqueduct: and that is the reafon, as I take it, that Spain in their time contained many millions more than it does in our days, as the foil, fecundated by various waters branching over all its provinces, produced food enough to maintain much larger numbers than it does at prefent. The fame may

may be said of several other regions, which were in those days the pride of the world, as history tells us, and lie now little less than depopulated. The aquisition of the best province in France, would possibly not add so much to the intrinsic power of Spain, as an aqueduct like that at Segovia, extending through the internal parts of the kingdom for only fifty leagues.

About three miles from Frejus we began to ascend several successive and encreasing eminencies during two hours; then descended for two hours more, which brought us to the small town of *Cannes*, where we halted to dine. It is not possible to give a true idea of the beauty of those hills, partly cultivated and partly wild. 'Tis a delicious tract, that offers numberless romantic prospects. Amongst the various plants and shrubs that grow spontaneously on all sides of those hills, the most remarkable is a kind of laurel, which produces a

most

most beautiful berry, about as big as a nut, of a form perfectly globular, pea-green when unripe, and scarlet-red when full-grown. Its rind is full of speckles, like a strawberry, and you cannot imagine how charming it looks when in the glory of perfect maturity. I am ignorant of its name, having never seen it before. Our clergyman says it is quite common all over the hills of Andalusia, where they call it *Madroño*, and adds, that the vulgar there have a notion the eating much of it would make one drunk. Yet I eat about a dozen without perceiving any such effect; but found it tasteless as well as harmless. Was this plant introduced in domestic gardens, it would prove no small embellishment at this time of the year.

From the windows of the inn at *Cannes*, we saw the small *Isle of Sainte Marguerite*, defended by a fortress, in which many state-criminals have ended their

their days in wretched confinement. After dinner, following the shore, we came to this town of *Antibes*, and at the gate we entered, were obliged to give a very strict account of ourselves to an officer deputed for the purpose of examining every goer and comer in this time of suspicion, as some English ships have appeared near the *Isles of Hieres*, and given a hot alarm to this whole coast.

Antibes is situated on a neck of land, which runs out into the sea, and becomes a kind of peninsula. The open sea breaks against its southern side: on the western is a large bay, in which any fleet may ride safe against the land-winds: the eastern side, which looks towards *Nice*, is formed into a very good harbour by the help of a long mole built with large stones; and a chain of hills surrounds the town on the north.

Those hills are very fruitful, and yield vast quantities of the best wine and

oil;

oil; but they have so absolute a command over the town, as would render its spacious fortifications of little use, was Antibes vigorously besieged by land. A battery of only twenty guns, would, I think, demolish in a very few days the three great bastions on that side, in spight of the high cavaliers over them, and the castle with four small bastions that has been erected opposite to the harbour. I am surprised how in the late war, the German troops, in conjunction with ours, missed the taking of it after having been for several days in possession of those hills. I suppose that the want of proper artillery caused the miscarriage of that enterprize.

Our baggage has been just now taken on board a felucca which we have hired for *Genoa*, and the governor has promised us our passports and certificates of health against to-morrow. Please God that the wind may cease during this night, together with the heavy rain that has accompanied us from *Cannes* to this place. I am impatient to row away for *Nice*, and tread upon Italian ground. We might eafily be there by to-morrow-night, as the paffage is not fixteen miles over. But a mighty ftorm, which has been raging thefe four and twenty hours, may poffibly keep us here fome days; nor was it poffible for us to go by land, as news were brought here this morning, that the bridge over the river *Var*, which feparates our king's dominions from France, has been broken laft night by a moft impetuous flood from the mountains.

LETTER LXXXIV.

A short, but frightful navigation. A dangerous cobler. Timely assistance. Montalban and Villafranca. *A fine valley. Simplicity of a youth from* St. Remo.

Nice, Nov. 14, 1760.

I Have been once or twice in danger of my life on my various rambles through several countries, but never yet have seen death stare me so full in the face as yesterday in the afternoon after we had left *Antibes,* and while we were making for *Nice* in a felucca, which was rowed by twelve men.

It was near noon when we got out of that harbour, the wind having abated much of that violence with which it had raged the whole night long. 'Tis true that the sea ran still very high, and that *Padrón Antonio,* the master of the felucca, was of opinion it would be better not to set out until it was quite appeased:

appeafed: but an abfurd fit of impatience made me infift on our departure, and foolifhly bribe his confent to my defire by means of an additional *Louis-d'or*.

We had not gone quite four miles; when a moft furious *Libeccio*, or southwind, came upon us, rolling fuch waves againft the land, as made our men look thoughtful, and row on in the faddeft filence.

I will not make my page magnificent with a defcription of the ftorm in which we were taken, and by which we expected every moment to be overwhelmed. It is enough to fay, that by tugging hard for three hours, and endeavouring to keep our diftance from the fhore, we arrived in fight of *Nice*. By the help of my fpying-glafs I faw the fides of the harbour there thronged with people, who, as I was told afterwards, ftood gazing at us, all perfuaded that we fhould foon break againft a rock called

the

the Cobler, (il Ciabattino) which lies about half a mile from the harbour, as they faw that the wind drove us forcibly towards it, and that we had not a fufficient number of hands to carry ourfelves out of the direction in which we were.

But what made our cafe look paft all hope, was, that thofe people, unable to conceive how any body could be fo daring as to leave *Antibes* during that perverfe weather, took it into their heads that we could not be but a part of the crew of fome *Barbary*-pirate feparated by fome accident from our fhip. Upon this fuppofition they imagined that we had refolved to make for the land at all events, and abandon ourfelves to an inevitable captivity, rather than to perifh by keeping in fo fmall a boat at an untenable diftance from the fhore.

With this conceit, which prefently prevailed amongft them all, none of them entertained for a while the leaft thought

thought of putting off to our affiftance, as they would otherwife have done if they had had any means of gueffing that we were not what they took us to be. Confidered therefore as a fmall number of African robbers, we were left to our own fhifts, becaufe it is always taken for granted all along this coaft, that the *Barbary*-pirates conftantly carry the plague on board; and upon that prefumption no body will ever venture out in their favour, whenever it happens (which is but feldom) that any fmall bark of theirs is feen at any little diftance in fuch diftrefs as we were; no body being willing to fubject himfelf to a tedious quarantine, which would be inevitable, were they only to fpeak to any bark not provided with a *certificate of health*, and efpecially to one belonging to any of the piratical nations.

Padron Antonio, who gueffed at all this, had but very faint hopes of deliverance from his danger; yet ftood waving

waving his hat as foon as he thought that we might be feen from fhore, and thus endeavoured to bring fome body to his fuccour. But the foulnefs of the weather, and the rifing and falling of the waves, would not for a while permit the people on fhore to have a full fight of us, which kept them long from ftirring in our behalf, and we were all the time approaching very faft toward that place that was to be our unavoidable deftruction. It pleafed God at laft, that they could diftinguifh our European dreffes, efpecially Cornacchini's red coat trimmed with fome gold. The inftant they were certain we were not Africans, a bark with four and twenty rowers put out towards us, and our men who faw them coming, recovered heart enough to tug harder and harder, to keep the felucca from running fo faft as it did againft that ugly *Cobler*. The bark reached us when we were not forty yards from our mortal enemy. The end of a rope was flung to us, which we luckily caught at the firſt throw, and preſently faſtened round our maſt. Had we miſſed it, we had been undone the next minute. Our deliverers rowed furiouſly back the way they had come, and their fotce, joined to ours, dragg'd us inſtantly away from the terrible rock. We ruſh'd into the mouth of the harbour tied to each other, to the great ſurpriſe of ſeveral hundred ſpectators, whoſe clamour, cries, and joy were very great as we went in. The Health-Officers were ſollicitous in their inſpection of our Certificates, and preſently permitted us to ſet foot upon land. The multitude crowded about us, ſome ſhaking hands with us, ſome embracing and kiſſing us, ſome chiding *Padron Antonio* for his leaving *Antibes* on ſo frightful a day, and all congratulating us upon our wonderful eſcape. We were carried in ſedans to the neareſt inn, and put immediately to bed, as, beſides the fright,

we

we had been utterly difcompofed by the great agitation of the water, which had made us all moſt piteouſly fea-fick. The Andaluſian Clergyman and Batifte, looked like fenfelefs fpectres: Cornacchini and his fervant had both vomited blood; and I could ſtand no longer on my legs. However, after two hour's reſt we found ourfelves fo well recovered, that we could fwallow fome broth: then fell into a ſleep, which for my part was not very quiet, as the hateful image of the foaming *Cobler* never would ceafe to prefent itfelf to my imagination.

This morning, as we were at breakfaſt, we received a viſit from fome of our ſtout deliverers, who in their own and their companions' name, congratulated us upon our happy efcape. Cornacchini and I made them fuch a prefent, as convinced them we were thankful for the activity they had exerted in our favour; and wifhed it had been in our

power

power to bestow a still greater reward. They appeared perfectly satisfied as it was: but as to our good Andalusian, I am sorry to say, that his goodness *begins not at the hands*, as we phrase it; and it is in vain the Pope reminds us with the inscription on his coin, that *melius est dare quam accipere*. The man is very meek and very humble: He mutters prayers almost the whole day long, and should be very glad to have us join with him in reciting rosaries and litanies; but liberality I have not yet found out to be one of his virtues, though, as to gratitude, he cannot in the present case be charged with the want of, because the sea-sickness had tormented him so much during the danger, that he was quite insensible of it, nor is he willing to take our word for it, as he would be something the poorer by believing. I should not chuse him for my travelling companion in a journey round the world, notwithstanding his great holiness.

This

This day has been very fine, and the sun has shone very bright: yet the sea not being quite so smooth as we could wish, we did not think proper to take to our Felucca, especially as all our throats are still very sore from our strainings in vomiting. I went on a mule this morning up a high hill opposite to the town, to give a look to the *Castle of Montalban* situated on its top. One might well call it a square tower, rather than a fortress, as it has no bastions, nor such deep ditches as a Fortress ought to have. Yet the difficulty of going up to it, makes it be considered as a strong one; and it was with a considerable loss of men that the French took it in the last war. On the east side of it, and much below it on the sea-shore, there is the citadel, the town, and the harbour of *Villafranca,* all commanded by that small thing, *Moutalban*'s Castle. The valley betwixt *Montalban* and *Nice* is one of the plea-
santest

fanteft that can be feen, thickly planted with olive and fruit-trees, and full of habitations; chiefly country-houfes belonging to the people of *Nice*. *Nice* had formerly another fortrefs adjoining, which having fallen after a long and bloody fiege into the hands of the French, was not only difmantled by order of Luis XIV, but the ftones that formed its walls carried away to *Antibes*, and employed in augmenting its fortifications. That King of warlike memory, play'd us many fuch tricks, and deftroyed no lefs than ten of the Citadels we had then in various parts of our King's dominions. Yet we have been ever fince building fo many new ones, that whenever the French fhall take it into their heads to come upon us, we fhall always find them bufinefs enough.

The air of *Nice* and the hills that environ it, is confidered as one of the very beft for confumptive people to breath. This notion, which I fuppofe fupported

by

by experience, is the cause that many strangers afflicted with that disorder, resort here from time to time. But *Nice* is so ugly a town, and affords so small a number of amusements, that nothing, I think, but the desire of preserving life, could induce me to come and live here. .

We dined *à table ronde* to-day with some gentlefolks that are just come from *St. Remo*, a town on this coast which belongs to the Genoese. Amongst them there was a young man, whose sweet manners did not escape my notice, and I made him my companion during the afternoon in a long walk. As we were returning to the inn, talking of our Italian Poets, in which he seems tolerably well versed, he stopped his words short, and stood looking with a remarkable surprise at a coach, that was going by from the town towards the harbour.

Are

Are you acquainted, said I, with the ladies in that coach, that you gaze upon them so intently?

And is that, answered he, what you call a coach?

To be sure, said I: but did you never see one before?

Never in my life, said he; as I never yet quitted my native place; and this is the first step that I have taken out of it. I am come with my parents to fetch a relation, who is to go back with us to *St. Remo*.

Though the coach was a very plain one, yet as we saw it stop, and the Ladies in it get out to walk, we went to inspect it, and I explained to him the use of its parts as well and as minutely as I could, very much to his satisfaction. I had never thought before that there could be a man in Italy who had reached the age of twenty, and yet never seen a coach.

From

From this town I might as well go over the great hill of *Tenda*, and through *Cuneo* and *Raconigi* to Turin: but there is too much fnow already on that hill, as I am told; therefore fhall ftick to the fcheme of coafting it along with *Padron Antonio* as far as Genoa, and find my way home from thence through *Alexandria* and *Cafál*. 'Tis a longer way, but lefs difficult.

LETTER LXXXV.

Gunpowder under water. Nice *no great rival to* Genoa *and* Leghorn. *Spanifh veracity, French lies, and French urbanity.*

Monaco, Nov. 15, 1760.

I Spent almoft the whole morning in looking at fome workmen employed in breaking a rock that lies almoft in the middle of the harbour of *Nice*. Tho' that

that rock is quite hidden under water, yet they have a method there of boring holes into it about a fpan deep, as I was told, and filling them with gunpowder. As that operation is inceffantly repeated, and the gunpowder lighted by means of a tube as foon as a hole is made and filled, the rock will foon be fhattered all to pieces, and the harbour rendered capable of admitting larger fhips than it does at prefent, which of courfe will encreafe the trade of the town, that has been declared a free port not many years ago.

Nice however will never be a formidable rival to the two neighbouring freeport-towns of *Genoa* and *Leghorn*, whatever privileges the fovereign may heap upon it, becaufe of the long chain of fteep mountains that lie on the back of it, and make the carriage of merchandizes too dear to and from Piedmont, and the other dominions of our King: nor has the County of *Nice* any commodities

modities of its own in such abundance, as to furnish a considerable trading-stock to its inhabitants, except oil and wine, which yet, though excellent in their respective kinds, are not in quantities large enough to afford cargoes for many merchantships.

About three this afternoon, the sea being quite calm, we rowed out from *Nice* for this *Monaco*, turning round a cape that juts so far into the sea, as to treble the distance between the two towns by water, which by land and over the hills is only three miles.

It was so late when we got here, that we could not go up to see the town, which is built on the elevated crest of a barren promontory; but were obliged to take our quarters at an inn by the harbour's side. If we do not set out too early to-morrow, I shall probably tell you something more of this place: but mean while, by way of lengthening this night's letter, and of filling up half an hour,

hour, let me take a retrospection of the country I have crossed since I quitted the Pirenees, and, like a true Traveller, descant a little upon the most observable qualities of its inhabitants.

I have often heard it repeated, that the French are naturally a chearful people; and this notion prevails so much amongst us, that I am almost afraid lest I expose myself to your ridicule by contradiction. But am I not intitled to speak my opinion upon this subject as much as any of my travelling predecessors, after having crossed the kingdom in various directions, and made some stay at different times both in its Capital and in other parts of it?

It may proceed from want of sagacity, but indeed I never was able to discover so universal a propension to hilarity in the people of France as is generally pretended, and such as may entitle them to the appellation of chearful by way of characteristick.

There is to be sure a difference easily observable between the French I have seen this fortnight past, and those who live in the opposite Provinces. The Languedocians and Provencials have certainly upon the whole such countenances, as bespeak a greater flow of spirits, than, for instance, the Normans and the Picardians. Yet that the French in general are in reality more chearful by nature than their neighbours, is not discoverable by external demonstration; and were I asked my opinion about the superiority in this particular between the Spaniards and them, I should not hesitate a moment to say, that the Spaniards have it by many degrees, as I have seen them actuated by it much oftener than the French.

Travel through Spain, as I have lately done; and, at night at least, 'tis ten to one that you alight at a house, where people disclose their chearfulness by singing and dancing; and those must undoubtedly

doubtedly be reckoned moſt chearful who ſhow it moſt. Almoſt every creature in Spain can handle a guittar and the caſtanets, and there is not one in a hundred but can ſhake his heels at the ſound. The *Fandango* and the *Seguedilla*, which are their national dances, you ſee danced every day, every where, and by every body; whereas the national dance of the French, which may be the *Minuet* for what I know, you may croſs their country backwards and forwards twenty times, and ſcarcely ever meet with a circle of peaſants and people of the lower claſſes practiſing it; nor have they any muſical inſtrument univerſally in vogue in any part of the kingdom, except in Provence, the only province in which you ſee with ſome ſort of frequency the ruſtick aſſemblies rouſed up to chearfulneſs by the *Fifre* and the *Tambourin*.

If the acts that are ofteneſt repeated by the greateſt number in any country,

are

are to be deemed as characteriftical of the nation that inhabits it, I fhould be tempted to fay, that one of the moft remarkable characterifticks of the French, at leaft of the bulk of them; that is, of the inferior claffes, is rather lying than chearfulnefs. It is no lefs aftonifhing than offenfive to fee how much this paultry vice prevails amongft them in all thofe parts of their kingdom that I have vifited. Go to buy any thing at any fhop, and you may be fure that the fhopman, his wife, his fon, his daughter, his apprentice, his man, his maid, every foul about him, will fwear *upon honour, upon faith,* or *upon truth,* that the thing you want cofts him *twenty,* though he will let you have it for *ten,* if you have but the patience to let him lower the price, which he will do in a few minutes. The moft frivolous enquiry is generally anfwered with a lye at an inn or the poft-houfe; and never once did I fit at any *table ronde,* but I was forced to take notice, that even people who looked like gentlemen by their tupees and ruffles, were tainted with this vice. 'Tis true that their ordinary lies are of the petty and uselefs kind; but still they are lies to all intents and purposes, and commonly so very glaring, as the tellers must be sensible it is impossible for the grossest credulity to swallow them for truths: yet such long strings of them have I seen reciprocally exchanged during a dinner, and delivered with such a serenity of impudence, as is unexampled in any other country, so far as I have as yet carried my observations.

That the number of petty liars is great in every country, no body will deny who has watched mankind with any degree of attention. But I must say thus much in honour of the Spaniards, that they have a greater regard for truth than any nation I have as yet visited. They have it proverbial, that *el Español no dice mentira,* " The Spaniard tells no
" lie;"

"*lie;*" and by much the greatest part of them stick to the proverb, as far as I could see in my present journey.

But that you may not conclude, from the severity of my remark about this characteristick of the French, that my long stay in England has infected me with that foolish antipathy towards them, which is there so universal; I must tell you, that, as the world goes, I am far from thinking the French more disagreeable than any other nation. Their lying to be sure creates a disgust in travellers that could never be overcome, was it not overballanced by many good qualities, which prevail throughout France in a greater degree than in any other of the countries I have as yet seen.

The reputation that the French have of being the most polished nation in Europe, I think is very well deserved by that universal complaisance, officiousness, and respect which they constantly practife both amongſt themſelves and to any foreigner that viſits their country. There is a pliancy in their manners, a ſtudy to pleaſe, a readineſs to be pleaſed, an apparent defire of being uſeful, that contributes much to make a man paſs the day with eaſe and ſatisfaction. The French can careſs you without affection, can flatter you without eſteem, and can ſerve you without the leaſt view to their own intereſt; and all this they will do with a freedom, with a promptitude, and above all with ſuch a ſhow of kindneſs, that muſt captivate the moſt ſhy, and put in good humour the moſt peeviſh.

How canſt thou admire the French (you will be apt to ſay) for ſuch qualities as theſe? For a goodneſs that is not goodneſs, as it has not its ſource in their hearts and their judgment?

Fair and ſoftly, my dear friends, and be not haſty to condemn without firſt hearing

hearing what I have to say in support of my admiration, and even approbation of French manners.

You will easily allow, I suppose, that such is the infirmity of human nature, as not to leave a possibility, even to the most honest, to love a great many with any great degree of ardour, and to act with respect to numbers in consequence of a true impulse of love.

This granted, I think myself in the right when I say, that the French are to be much valued on account of their general character of politeness, or urbanity, call it as you like best. What can they do more, than act with all mankind near as well as any body would with his bosom-friend? Am I not to be more thankful for a kindness bestowed upon me without any previous reason, than for one extorted in a manner by friendship, expectation, real merit, or some other such powerful motive? And is it not very humane to treat an utter stranger with

with a goodnefs, which, though not derived from true love, yet anfwers the fame, or nearly the fame purpofe, and makes me nearly as happy for the time? A very wretched world this would be, were no body to be kindly treated but in confequence of known merit and previous love! The French nation has therefore a very juft claim to my refpect and praife, whofe individuals have fo ftrong an habit of urbanity, as to be kind to any body, without troubling themfelves about fcrupulous diftinctions of merit and defect, and confulting only the general intereft of mankind.

LETTER LXXXVI.

A dwarfifh kingdom, and its contents.

Monaco, Nov. 16, 1760.

THIS is a ftormy feafon, and by a ftorm which has raged the whole day, we have been kept here in fpight of ourfelves: yet I am very glad it did

not

not catch us at sea like the last, the terror of which has scarcely had time to subside. The wind has now abated much of its fury, and the sky is grown clear again; but we must see the waves quite flat before we dare to venture out in so small a thing as our felucca.

This delay has put it in my power to tell you something of this place, which I had otherwise left unobserved.

Monaco, as I told you yesterday, is seated on a rock so barren, that it has given rise to the rhymed saying,

> *Son Monaco sopr' uno scoglio:*
> *Non semino, e non ricoglio:*
> *Eppure mangiar voglio.*

In English, "*I am Monaco seated on a* "*rock. Neither do I sow, nor gather any* "*thing; yet I will not starve.*" The last line seems to reflect commendation on the industry of the inhabitants.

The principality, of which *Monaco* is the capital, lies between a ridge of mountains

mountains little lefs than perpendicular, the higheft parts of which are quite naked; but the loweft are almoft always green, being moiftened by droppings from the rocks, and overfhadowed by numberlefs trees, amongft which are the olive and the lemon, befides a few vines fcattered here and there.

The ftate extends fomething lefs than feven miles from *Monaco* eaftward, and is not quite a mile broad where it is broadeft. The town of *Monaco* might eafily be infulated by cutting off a fmall neck, which joins it to the land. It is fortified and garrifoned by a French battalion. I cannot conceive what need this prince has for foldiers, whofe commander is not dependant on his orders. Neither our king, nor the Genoefe, who are his only neighbours, ever laid any claim to his diminutive empire, nor can ever think it worth while to take it from him. Should that once be the cafe, with regard to our king efpecially,

of

of what use would that garrison be? The town and the whole principality would soon be reduced, as the high parts of the mountain belong to the county of *Nice*, and from thence *Monaco* might be pelted into a surrender.

This morning by break of day I went to pay my visit to that small metropolis, ascending a steep path paved with bricks, which cannot be trod but by men and asses. Horses and mules are forbid it, least they should spoil it with their shoes.

You may well think that my visit was soon ended, as the town contains but little more than two hundred small houses, which form four or five short streets. I had been told last night, that there was no gallows, as the inhabitants never commit any crime worth hanging. But one part of the assertion did not prove true, and one of the first objects that presented on one of the ramparts, was a pair of gallows built with bricks.

bricks. However, they were in a moſt ruinous condition, and it appears that they have not been fit for ſervice theſe many years.

The two principal buildings in the town (beſides the prince's palace) are two churches, one of which has a nunnery, where about a dozen girls are boarded by as many nuns. Both edifices are proportionate to the town, and one would rather call them little chapels.

As to the prince's palace, it is a fabrick which would not diſgrace any town in Italy. The walls on the outſide are painted, and repreſent ſoldiers clad in iron-armour. The air of Monaco is ſo pure, that it has not damaged thoſe figures, though they have been painted this century at leaſt. I am told that there are ſeveral grand apartments in it, very nobly furniſhed and decorated with ſome pictures by our moſt famed maſters. As it ſtands on the brink of a high rock, you have from its windows an
extenſive

extenfive profpect of the fea, as well as over the dominions of its owner.

Monaco, however, is not the only town in thefe dominions. There is *Mentone* on the further extremity of the country, which is a much larger town than *Monaco* itfelf, and contains above a thoufand inhabitants more. At *Mentone* the prince has another palace, befides a country-houfe by the village of *Roccabruna*, which ftands mid-way between *Mentone* and *Monaco*.

The prefent fovereign, who lives in France, and is a duke and peer of that realm under the title of *Valentinois*, comes from time to time to pay a vifit to his fubjects here, and you cannot imagine how he makes them happy whenever he comes. No fubjects love their prince more than thefe, and with very good reafon, as he never lays any tax on them. The only one they have, is the thirteenth part of their annual product; and as it is at their option to pay it either in kind or

in

in money, you may well fee that it cannot prove heavy.

The whole principality being but four miles fquare, one would be apt to imagine that the thirteenth part of its produce muft form but a very indifferent income: yet it is a fact that fuch income amounts to no lefs than a hundred thoufand French livres. So great is the difference between fuch lands as ours about Turin and this territory. Twenty of our acres there, are not worth one here, becaufe thefe produce olive-trees, each of which is worth a field fown with corn or with any thing elfe.

The produce of that narrow fuperficies, with the addition of what is fupplied by the fea, and by fome little traffick, maintains all the inhabitants of this fmall corner of the world, none of whom has a needy look, though none can be termed rich; the richeft burgefs in *Monaco*, as I am told, poffeffing but forty pounds income. Yet their number amounts to fix thoufand;

thoufands; that is, two in *Monaco*, three in *Mentone*, about five hundred in *Roccabruna*, and as many fcattered about in houfes and cots.

The coins here current, are the French, the Piedmontefe, and the Genoefe, befides their own. Of this I have by me a *liard*, a *fou*, and a *piéce de douze fous*. The *liard* and the *fou* are of copper, and the *piéce* is of filver. This *piéce* has on one fide the prince's effigy with the words round *D. G. Prin. Monoeci*; that is, " *by the grace of God Prince of Monaco*. The prince's arms occupy the reverfe with the legend round, *Dux Valent. Par. Franciæ*; that is, " *Duke of Valentinois* " *Peer of France*." I am told that there is alfo the *Piece of four and twenty fous* of filver, and the *gold piftole*, which is worth *four and twenty French* livres: but thefe two I could not procure, becaufe no coin is here fo fcarce as their own, the prince having no mint, and being obliged to have it made in France, which he has not chosen to do these many years.

As the rain has lasted the whole morning, I was obliged to make use of an umbrello in my walk over the greatest part of this state. That walk I performed along a fine coach-road the prince has lately caused to be made from *Monaco* to *Mentone*, close by the sea-shore, for the convenience of his princess, who, when she is here, rides in the only coach that ever was seen in the country. Between them both they have a guard of twenty men dressed in scarlet trimmed with silver, and in that number consists the whole of his army. As to his navy, it is somewhat more considerable, being composed of two barks, or ships, call them as you list, one of which carries forty men armed with muskets and cutlasses; the other three score men with eight swivels. A pigmy force, you will say: yet it is sufficient to put under contribution every thing that swims in sight; and there is no bark nor ship of inferior force, that would dare to row or sail in those seas without paying a certain small tax, which this prince has an acknowledged right to levy towards the maintenance of the several lights he keeps along the shore for the convenience of navigation. Our felucca, which is armed only with half a dozen rusty knives just able to slice a loaf, could not escape paying the tax, and *Padron Antonio* was obliged to disburse twenty French *sous* as he entered this port, which might with more propriety be termed a pond, if it had not one of its sides open to the sea that supplies it with a shallow water.

I suppose you will smile at this account, as it is almost impossible to refrain upon hearing of things of the dwarfish kind. But how proud would you be, were you absolute sovereign of any empire ever so diminutive? Contemptible as this of Monaco may appear when compared with that of the ancient Romans,

Affyrians, or Macedonians, yet not even the greateft mind will be apt to think it fo, upon turning a moment to the numberlefs millions that are not poffeffed of a fingle fpan of this globe's fuperficies; and I have already told you, that the fuperficies of this empire is more than a fpan fince it is near four miles fquare.

But jefting afide, there are few tracts of land that rejoice the fight fo much as this. This foil, covered with a variety of plants, forms a fine contraft with the barren cliffs that border it on one fide, and with the wide liquid expanfe that runs along on the other; and there is a brook that falls down the mountain near *Roccabruna*, which one could gaze upon with pleafure for more than half an hour.

But I hear a centinel from the rampart cry out *Prenez garde à vous*; and I muft *prendre garde à moi* and go to bed, as the night is already far advanced.

I ought not to omit saying, that the language of this people is an odd dialect, half Provencial and half Genoese. Yet a great many of them speak French, which is taught them by the soldiers of the garrison. The university of *Monaco* is comprised in a grammar-school. I have not had time to inform myself of the laws of the country, and the manner in which justice is administered.

LETTER LXXXVII.

A chapel singularly adorned. No adventure at sea. Sea-geese. Anchises carrying Eneas. Bite not with feeble teeth. Modest women.

St. Remo, Nov. 17, 1760.

THE air was so quiet this morning, the sky so clear, and the sea so gentle, that we rowed away from *Monaco* by seven o'clock, after having heard a mass in a chapel about half a mile distant from the inn. The inside of that chapel is oddly adorned with chains, fetters, swords, sabres, cutlasses, firelocks, and pistols, hung there by way of *Ex Voto*'s. It is dedicated to *Santa Divota*, a holy dame, whose name I don't remember to have read in the *Roman Martyrology*. She is the patroness of the little monarchy, and is very miraculous, as all saints are in little places: witness those many instuments of misery and death in her chapel, which by her powerful intercession did no hurt to those who hung them there.

As we coasted along close to the land, we saw *Lete*, a pretty village, just by the town of Ventimiglia, the episcopal jurisdiction of which extends over some part of the county of *Nice*, though belonging to a different sovereign.

At *Lete*, which is not two miles from *Mentone*, begins the country of the Genoese. *Ventimiglia* is surrounded with fortification, but in so feeble a manner,

that

that in the laſt war our troops took it in leſs than a week.

We arrived here at three in the afternoon. As *St. Remo* has no harbour, the felucca was run aground upon a ſandy bank, and our mariners carried us aſhore on their ſhoulders. Thus ended this day's navigation, which was only forty miles, attended by no adventure good or bad, except that of finding a fir-tree, which *Padron Antonio* gueſſes to have been rooted out and carried down the mountains by the *Ventimiglia*-river, that has been much ſwelled by the late rains, and rendered very impetuous.

We ſaw the track of that river, extending a full mile from the ſhore; and we diſtinguiſhed its water from that of the ſea by its progreſſive motion, but ſtill more by the great quantity of moſs, leaves, and broken boughs that covered it. A multitude of *Oche d' acqua*, or *Sea-geeſe*, hovered over that track, and plunged to peck, I know not what kind of food. The *Oca d' acqua* is a fine bird, as far as I could fee, and has its name from the refemblance it bears to a common goofe. Had we had a mufket, we might eafily have killed fome. They are very good eating, fays *Padron Antonio*. When he took me up to carry me on fhore, he put me in mind of a picture, that would contraft very well with that of Eneas carrying his aged father, becaufe *Padron Antonio* is about as old as I fuppofe Anchifes was when his fon ran away with him from the burning town, and I am probably not older than the Trojan hero. Excufe the comparifon between a hero and your brother, as I muft write whatever comes uppermoft when the argument proves fcanty.

St. Remo is one of the moft pleafing places on the Ligurian coaft. Upon the whole it is well built, and makes a fine appearance from the fea. They fay that it has above twelve thoufand inhabitants, whofe chief revenue chiefly arifes from the

the sale of their oranges and lemons, which grow on the hills round the town. A thousand of them generally sell on the spot for two Genoese livres, (eighteen pence sterling) and I leave you to judge of the quantities that must be sold to support a place so populous: nor is it permitted them to send any out of the country, that do not pass through an iron-ring, which the magistrates produce at the time of the gathering. Those that have outgrown the ring, are supposed to be too ripe for transportation.

Amongst the houses of *St. Remo* the most showy is one belonging to the family of the *Boria*'s, the most opulent in the town. That house is so large, that it contains just as many windows as there are days in the year when it is not bissextile. At least the inhabitants tell you so; and I took their word for it, rather than to be at the trouble of counting them. A strange whim of the gentleman who caused it to be built. Should the government

vernment lay a window-tax as it does in England, his heirs would probably think it advantageous to demolish it. They say that he had a brother, who took great pains to know the exact number of confessionals that are in the churches at Rome. 'Tis difficult to determine who was the idler of the two.

While dinner was making ready at the inn, I went to take a tour through the town, and the best thing I saw in it was a little church belonging to the nuns of the order of *the Visitation*. It has three altars made of the finest marbles. The church of the Jesuits is also very pretty, and neatly ornamented. In a garden I saw many palm-trees, which make a pleasing appearance with their variegated leaves: but the climate is not hot enough to make them produce dates as in Africa. The people of *St. Remo* have long enjoyed the privilege of furnishing Rome with palms on Palm-sunday, and are under an engagement to send a cargo

thither

thither every year. Should they fail once, the privilege would be forfeited: but as long as they fulfil the engagement, the privilege is to be exclufive, which brings them fome thoufand of * *Scudi* every year.

Between the town and the fea-fhore the Genoefe have lately built a fmall fortrefs to bridle this people, who not long ago took into their heads to revolt againft the republick, on pretence that their liberties were encroached upon, and a tax laid, which, as they pretended, the republick had no right to levy. But the confequence of their revolt proved fatal to many of them, that were taken and fent to the gallies. A body of Genoefe troops foon fubdued them, and obliged feveral of the moft opulent inhabitants to quit the country, who left their patrimony behind to be confifcated. The outlaws are now foliciting redrefs at

* *A* Scudo *is about five fhillings fterling.*

Vienna;

Vienna; but will probably find none, as their town and territory is too inconfiderable to attract the attention of that court. They have now found by woeful experience, that they would have done better to keep quiet and pay the tax, which the republick could not help laying, after it had been exhaufted by us and the Germans in the laft war. Before we attempt to fhow our teeth, we ought in prudence to feel them, and fee whether they are ftrong enough to bite to any purpofe; but this is what this people did not think of; which has rendered their condition much worfe than it would otherwife have been, as the new fortrefs will for ever empower their mafters to act as they fhall think proper, and without much minding ancient liberties and worn-out rights.

In fpight however of their late misfortunes, I have fcarcely feen any where a people look fo well as this. Their habiliments are in general very clean, and

and I admire much the head-dress of their women, which consists of nothing else but a red silk riband about two inches broad, tied round the head, and formed into a large knot over the forehead. The hair they wear in hanging tresses, combed very clean. Though the fashion is simple, it gives the handsome an air of alertness, and many of them are handsome. An honest lemon-merchant, to whom my little friend at *Nice* gave me a line of recommendation, told me, that there are no women in the world so modest and so good as these; and I am inclined to believe him when I consider that luxury, the great parent of vice, has not yet found her way hither, nor is likely ever to find it, as *St. Remo* and its territory are encompassed on one side by the sea, and on the other by a rugged mountain; so that they stand in a manner separated from the rest of the world.

LETTER LXXXVIII.

A felucca set a-float. Few people helped to their proper stations. Tonadilla's *sung. A long chain of habitations. A strong fortress.*

Savona, Nov. 18, 1760.

YESTERDAY, after we had been carried ashore on our mariners' shoulders, the felucca was likewise dragged out of the water, least a nightly swell of the sea should damage it, or carry it away. This morning therefore it was necessary to set it afloat before our departure: but the manner of performing that operation offered an object so very picturesque, that I could not forbear regretting my want of skill in the art of drawing, which kept me from making a very fine sketch. Imagine some of our Argonauts stooping down to excavate the sand before the felucca with their own hands for want of shovels,

shovels, that it might find an easy passage to the water; others putting planks and rollers under it to facilitate its sliding; some running their brawny shoulders and backs against its sides, some their heads, some their hips; all helping, all straining every nerve and muscle to effect their purpose. Their different ages, their contrasted attitudes, their distortions, the grinning faces they made while labouring thus hard, seemed to call for a picture, that would be well worth the vigorous pencil of my friend *Cipriani*. I wish he had been there; and indeed I wish him to be wherever I am.

While I stood gazing at our mariners thus violently employed, it came into my head that the satisfaction of a felucca would be very great, could a felucca but think, and be susceptible of satisfaction.

A felucca (thought I) is only serviceable when it is in the water: and that

it.

it may be placed where it is of ufe, fee how many hands are eager to afford their help! Is it not a great caufe of fatisfaction to be thus efficacioufly affifted, that we may be in the very place where we may prove ufeful? But why is this fo feldom the cafe with men? Few, very few, are the men, who ever find willing and powerful hands to pufh them into thofe ftations, in which they would prove of the greateft fervice to their fellow-creatures. Be thy abilities ever fo great, never art thou forcibly placed where thou oughteft to be. In vain has nature given thee powers fufficient to be a poet or a phyfician, an hiftorian or a ftatefman: thou art obliged to direct a plough, or carry a mufket, or ride behind in a livery, or do ftill fome meaner thing, becaufe no body thought of helping thee, and thrufting thee into thy proper element!

'Tis needlefs to tell you how far I carried this fpeculation, as you may
plunge

plunge into it yourselves now I have given you the hint, and push it so far as it will go. Yet think you how few they are, within the circle of your own observations, who ever were helped to stations suitable to their natural parts and powers. It is my opinion you will scarcely find one, who ever had the good luck that our felucca has had this morning.

We had not rowed a mile from *St. Remo*, when a soft breeze from the west made our men lay down their oars, and spread a sail, by which means we went thirty miles in little more than three hours. Thirty more remained to *Savona*; but an odious calm succeeding about noon, the poor fellows were again obliged to tug hard till sun-set. Had we not had Cornacchini with us, so slow a navigation would have proved irksome enough: but he has bought a guittar at *Nice*, and beguiles the tedious hours by playing and singing. No body that ever I heard,

I heard, warbles better *sotto voce* than Cornacchini; and the numberless *Siguedillas* and *Tonadillas*, which he has learned in Spain, have quite won him the heart of our grave Andalusian. I think I have already told you, that a *Tonadilla* is an odd sort of musical composition, partly sung in various measures, and partly spoken: but those couplets that are spoken, must be pronounced so, that the tone of the voice be concordant with the sound. Italy has no musick, that ever I heard, so truly joyous as a *Tonadilla*.

Besides this diversion I had also that of surveying the coast as we went along, as we did not chuse to lose sight of it for fear of a sudden change of the weather in this unsettled season. We would have it in our power to land whenever we should think it proper, as the memory of the cruel Cobler is still fresh in our minds. The world cannot boast of a more delightful country than the Ligurian state. It consists of nothing along this coaſt, but of rocks and cliffs when viewed from the ſea; but all ſo covered with inceſſant vegetation, as to be for ever green. I propoſed to count the towns and villages from *Ventimiglia* down to *Genoa*, but ſoon loſt my reckoning becauſe of their number. The whole coaſt looks little leſs than a continued town, ſo many are the inhabitants along it. Beginning in particular at *Porto Maurizio*, and ending at *Oneglia*, the populouſneſs is beyond belief, as within that ſpace, which is only five miles in length, upon a breadth of four miles, there are no leſs than forty villages, beſides thoſe two towns.

We landed here at *Savona* when the ſun was juſt ſetting, as I ſaid above, and went to lodge at a very good inn without the walls. If the weather continues quiet, we ſhall be gone to-morrow early, and without entering its gates; but without regret on my ſide, as I have already ſeen it ſome years ago. *Savona* is, next *Genoa,* the largeſt town of the republick. It had formerly a very capacious and ſafe harbour, that was in good meaſure filled up, and rendered unfit to receive large ſhips, becauſe it deprived that of Genoa of too great a part of its trade. The *Savoneſe* ſtill grumble at the injury they have ſuffered by the ſpoiling of their harbour : but, ſuppoſe that their town was the ſeat of power, inſtead of Genoa, how long do you think that the Genoa-harbour would ſubſiſt? It was intereſt, and not malignity, that induced the Genoeſe to order the deſtruction of the harbour of Savona : but intereſt always carries a malignant aſpect, when backed by power to the prejudice of others, and it is as natural for the *Savona*-people to hate that aſpect, as it is natural for their lords at *Genoa* to make the moſt of their power.

Savona is commanded by a citadel, the walls and ditches of which have been hewn out of the rock : yet in the laſt war

war our troops took it eafily. But as foon as our king had it in his poffeffion, and hopes given him that he fhould keep it for ever, he ordered the *Chevalier Pinto*, who had conducted the fiege, to fortify it to the beft of his fkill. The brave engineer reformed its numerous irregularities, raifed its walls with an overwork, deepened its ditches, and in fhort put it in fuch a condition, that it is now thought impregnable. I wifh it was, together with all the fortreffes in Europe, that fovereigns might think no more of war and of invading each other's dominions.

The town of *Savona* contains no lefs than thirty thoufand inhabitants, befides the five or fix thoufand in its fuburbs; and it is one of the beft built we have in Italy, abounding with noble houfes, large churches, ample hofpitals, and other kinds of public edifices. It has a fertile territory, feveral miles broad, and extending feven miles within land to a huge mountain, which I afcended once in two hours, riding on a mule. It was then winter-time, as it is now; and I have not yet forgot that I have fuffered much in that journey. The wind blew fo violent on the top of that mountain, that I was obliged to alight in various narrow paffes, for fear of being thrown down the precipices. What a horrible thing to travel over the cliffs of *Mezzanótt*, *Malavsín*, and *Cartóz* in ftormy weather, as was then my cafe! 'Tis a long chain of mountains, the northern fides of which were then covered with fheets of frozen fnow feveral miles broad. This is the reafon, that I abftain from taking the road through the *High Monferrat*, and ftifle the defire of feeing for the prefent our numerous relations and friends in various parts of that province. I know that my unexpected appearance amongft them would prove delightful, and am fure they would exhauft many a cafk to make me welcome. But the

feafon

feafon is by much too fevere on their fide for me to quit the felucca. I fhall fee them next fpring, and without putting myfelf to any great inconvenience.

LETTER LXXXIX.

The lies of the inn-keepers at Genoa. The laſt ſtage.

Genoa, Nov. 18, 1760.

WE came here from *Savona* in lefs than five hours, befriended by a gale of wind that feemed to blow by our own order. The horizon was fo bright by the time we approached this harbour, that we could leifurely enjoy the noble profpect a while, and take the whole town at one glance. What a magnificent femicircle! Nothing, they fay, can match it, but *Naples* and *Conſtantinople*. I had feen *Genoa* many times, but this day it has pleafed and furprifed me me full as much as ever. 'Tis really a glorious town.

Within thefe ten years that I have been abfent, I find the Genoefe have added two light-houfes to their harbour, by means of which its entrance on a dark night has been rendered much fafer. I could not refrain a figh on turning my eyes to thofe light-houfes, as I recollected that they were built upon occafion of the lofs of a fhip, in which a friend of mine was caft away. Poor *Guido Riviera!* We fhall recite no more verfes together!

Having fhowed our certificates of health at the out-houfe, we rowed forward to the landing place, where feveral inn-keepers waited for us to offer their fervice.

We will go to *Santa Marta*, faid Cornacchini to them : pleafe therefore not to importune us with your clamour.

That

That inn, anfwered one of them, has unluckily been burned down not a month ago: and fo, good firs, you may as well come to the *Croce di Malta*, where you will find good accommodations, and as kind a reception as any where elfe.

Had I been alone, I fhould have fallen into the fnare of the fmooth-tongued fellow. But Cornacchini, who knows better than I, infifted on our going to *Santa Marta*, and would only promife to be the fellow's gueft in cafe we fhould find no lodging there.

But, faid I, why will you be at the trouble of going to an inn that is no more?

Becaufe, faid he, I am fure that this man is a liar, and the inn not burnt down.

The reply was pretty fmart: yet gave no offence. - The fellow, inftead of fhowing refentment, only perfifted in his affertion, and fwore to it fo pofitively and with fuch an air of candour, that I

knew

knew not what to make of it: nor was it without reluctance that I yielded to Cornacchini's advice, and went to *Santa Marta*.

Cornacchini's guefs proved true; and on our arrival there I fhould have exclaimed long againft the matchlefs impudence of the fcoundrel, had not another fcoundrel ftopped me fhort. The *Santa Marta*-man made me forbear exclaiming, by telling me, that he was not at all furprifed at the man's lie. I have myfelf, faid he, burnt down his inn fo many times, that he would be a great fool if he miffed the opportunity of burning mine whenever he can. It is our common practice, added the wretch with the greateft fang-froid, to burn each other in this manner. Every body muft endeavour to draw the water to his own mill.

Your practice, faid I, is very laudable, no doubt. Yet 'tis pity you are not all fent to exercife it in a galley.

Pfhaw,

Pshaw, pshaw, replied the man: do not be out of humour with our frolicks. We will treat you very well.

I made haste to *Signor Paolo Celesia*, a worthy friend of mine, who has resided some years in England as minister of the republic, and married there a most amiable Englishwoman. Neither of them expected to see me, as they had had no intimation of my coming. With them, and some other old acquaintance, I passed a very agreeable evening. They would fain have persuaded me to stay here a few days: but I know that you must begin to be apprehensive of some accident, as I have been much longer about this journey than I proposed: besides that the vicinity of my native home makes me impatient of further delays. I shall therefore take post to-morrow by break of day, and hope to be with you at sun-set. After so long and happy a journey, we must to-morrow night sing together in

the

the full humility of our hearts, *Agimus tibi gratias, omnipotens Deus, pro univerfis beneficiis tuis, qui vivis et regnas in fecula feculorum.*

The END of the JOURNEY from LONDON to GENOA.

An APPENDIX

For the instruction of those who intend to travel to Madrid by land.

EVERY body knows, that there is no entering Spain from any part of France, but by crossing the Pirenees.

The roads through those mountains go under two different denominations with the Spaniards. Those which admit of wheel-carriages, they call *Caminos de Ruedas*; and *Caminos de Herradura* they term those, which are too narrow for such vehicles. A *Camino de Herradura* is generally travelled on a mule. Couriers only run it out on horseback, changing horses at different stages.

The best *Camino de Ruedas* through those mountains, is certainly that which I have described in the foregoing letters. But to spare my reader the trouble of tracing it out of them, I give it here again, beginning at *Perpignan*, which

is

is the chief town in the province of *Rouffillon*.

The ROAD
From *Perpignan* to *Madrid*.

	No. of leagues
From *Perpignan* to *Boulou*	5
From *Boulou* to *Bellegarde*	1
From *Bellegarde* to *Jonquiera*, which is the firſt place in Spain	1
From *Jonquiera* to *Hoſtal Nuevo*	2
From *Hoſtal Nuevo* to *Figuieras*	$1\frac{1}{2}$
From *Figuieras* to *Santa Locaya*	1
Here you croſs a river on a boat.	
From *Santa Locaya* to *Baſcara*	$1\frac{1}{2}$
From *Baſcara* to *Villa de Muls*	$\frac{1}{2}$
From *Villa de Muls* to *Medina*	2
A river croſſed over a bridge.	
From *Medina* to *Girona*	1
From *Girona* to *Hoſtal de Ceba*	1
From *Hoſtal de Ceba* to *Las Mallorquinas*	$2\frac{1}{2}$
From *Las Mallorquinas* to *Hoſtalrich*	2
From *Hoſtalrich* to *Batloria*	1
From *Batloria* to *Sanſeloni*	1
From *Sanſeloni* to *Linarez*	2
A river croſſed over a bridge.	
From *Linarez* to *La Roca*	1
From *La Roca* to *Monmelo*	1
From *Monmelo* to *Los Hoſtals*	1

Carried over   29

	No. of leagues
Brought over	29
From *Los Hoſtals* to *Moncada*	1
From *Moncada* to *Sant' Andrés*	1
From *Sant' Andrés* to BARCELLONA	1
From BARCELLONA to *Hoſpitalet*	1
From *Hoſpitalet* to *San Feliu*	$\frac{1}{2}$
From *San Feliu* to *Molin de Reys*	$\frac{1}{2}$
A river croſſed over a bridge.	
From *Molin de Reys* to *Sant' Andrea*	1
A river croſſed over a bridge.	
From *Sant' Andrea* to *Martorel*	1
From *Martorel* to *La Veguda*	1
From *La Veguda* to *Maqueſa*	1
From *Maqueſa* to *Piera*	1
From *Piera* to *Valbona*	$\frac{1}{2}$
From *Valbona* to *Puente de la Reyna*	$\frac{1}{2}$
A river waded.	
From *Puente de la Reyna* to *La Pobla*	1
The above river waded again.	
From *La Pobla* to *Villanoba*	$\frac{1}{2}$
From *Villanoba* to *Igualada*	$\frac{1}{2}$
From *Igualada* to *Yorba*	1
From *Yorba* to *Meſon del Gancho*	1
From *Meſon del Gancho* to *Santa Maria*	$\frac{1}{2}$
From *Santa Maria* to *Porcariſes*	$1\frac{1}{2}$
From *Porcariſes* to *Meſon Nuevo de Monmaneu*	$\frac{1}{2}$
From *Meſon Nuevo* to *Hoſtalets*	$1\frac{1}{2}$
From *Hoſtalets* to CERBERA	1
Carried over	49

	No. of leagues
Brought over	49
From CERBERA to *Curullada* - -	1
From *Curullada* to *Tarrega* - -	1
From *Tarrega* to *Villagrafa* - -	1
From *Villagrafa* to *Belpuch* - -	1
From *Belpuch* to *Gomez* - -	1
From *Gomez* to *Mollerufa* - -	1
From *Mollerufa* to *Belloch* - -	2

A river croffed over a bridge.

From *Belloch* to LERIDA - -	2
From LERIDA to *Alcaraz*, which is the laſt town in Catalonia - -	2

A river croffed over a bridge.

From *Alcaraz* to FRAGA, which is the firſt town in Aragon - -	3
From FRAGA to *Venta de Fraga* -	2
From *Venta de Fraga* to *Candafnos* -	2
From *Candafnos* to *Peñalba* - -	1½
From *Peñalba* to *Bujalaroz* - -	1½
From *Bujalaroz* to *Venta de Santa Lucia* -	3
From *Venta de Santa Lucia* to *Ofera* -	2
From *Ofera* to *Villafranca de Ebro* -	2
From *Villafranca* to *Alfajarin* - -	1
From *Alfajarin* to *Puebla de Alfinden* -	1

Two rivers croffed over bridges; that is, the Gallego, and the Ebro or Hebro.

From *Puebla* to ZARAGOZZA - -	3
From ZARAGOZZA to *Santa Fé* - -	1

Carried over 84

	No. of leagues
Brought over	84
From *Santa Fé* to *Maria*	1
From *Maria* to *Venta de Martorita*	1
From *Venta de Martorita* to *Venta de Mazota*	½
From *Venta de Mazota* to *La Muela*	½
From *La Muela* to *Longares*	3
From *Longares* to *Cariñena*	1
From *Cariñena* to *Venta de San Martin*	2
From *Venta de San Martin* to *Maynar*	1½
From *Maynar* to *Retafcon*	1
A river croffed over a bridge.	
From *Retafcon* to DAROCA	1
From DAROCA to *Ufed*, which is the laft town in Aragon	2
From *Ufed* to *Embid*	3
From *Embid* to *Tortuera*	1
From *Tortuera* to *Tartanedo*	2
From *Tartanedo* to *Concha*	1
From *Concha* to *Anchuela del Campo*, which is the laft town in the diftrict called *El Partido de Molina*	1
From *Anchuela del Campo* to *Barbacil*	2
From *Barbacil* to *Maranchon*	1
From *Maranchon* to *Aquilarejo*	2
From *Aquilarejo* to *Alcolea*, which is the laft town in the province or diftrict called *De Soria*	1
From *Alçolea* to *Torremocha*	2
From *Torremocha* to *Algora*	1

VOL. IV.   Q   Carried over 115½

	No. of leagues
Brought over	115½
From *Algora* to *Grajanejos*	4
From *Grajanejos* to *Triqueque*	2
From *Triqueque* to *Torrija*	1
From *Torrija* to *Valdenoches*	2
From *Valdenoches* to GUADALAXARA	1

A river crossed over a bridge. At that bridge the District (or *Partido*) *de Guadalaxara* ends, and that of *Alcárria* begins.

From GUADALAXARA to *Venta de San Juan*	2
From *Venta de San Juan* to *Venta de Meco*	1
From *Venta de Meco* to ALCALA' *de Henarez*, which is the first town in *New Castile*	1

Two small rivers waded.

From ALCALA' to *Torrejón de Ardóz*	2

Another small river waded.

From *Torrejon de Ardóz* to *Puente de Viveros*	1
From *Puente de Viveros* to *Rejas*	1
From *Rejas* to *Alameda*	½
From *Alameda* to *Canillejas*	½

A small river waded.

From *Canillejas* to MADRID.	1
Total of leagues from *Perpignan* to *Madrid*	135½

It is notorious, that there is no going post through any part of Spain in a wheel-carriage, but only on horseback, after

after the manner of the couriers. A courier told me in Spain, that there are no better horses in Europe for the purpose of riding post than those in Spain. Few gentlemen however would chuse to go in that manner; and he, who intends to go the above, or any other Spanish road, and does not chuse to ride on horseback, must either have his own carriage, and hire mules or horses to it, or hire both a carriage and mules at *Perpignan*, where this may always be done. Those who go the journey with their own voitures, will find it costly, as the calesseros or muleteers must in that case come back from *Madrid* to *Perpignan* to fetch their chaises; and it is plain that they must be paid both for the going and coming; which would not be the case if they took their chaises or coaches along with them, and have a chance left of bringing back some other traveller. The expence of a pair of mules and a man, will generally amount to twelve or thirteen shillings a day,

day, going at the rate of ten or eleven leagues. If you want to go faster, you must pay three or four shillings a day more; as in that case your conductors will be at the additional expence of changing mules at *Barcelona* and *Zaragozza*.

There are two other great roads, or *Caminos de Ruedas* through the Pirenees. One is from *Bayonne* to *Pamplona*; the other from *Bayonne* to *Vittoria*. Bayonne is the last considerable town in France on the side of *Biscay*; *Pamplona* is the capital of *Navarre*; and Vittoria (if I am not mistaken) is the chief town in the small province of *Alava*.

The ROAD
From *Bayonne* to *Pamplona*.

	No. of leagues
From BAYONNE to *Mediondo*	4
From *Mediondo* to San Juan Pie de Puerto	4
From *San Juan* to *Roncesvalles*	4
From *Roncesvalles* to *Burguete*	2
Carried over	14

	No. of leagues
Brought over	14
From *Burguete* to *Espinar*	1
From *Espinar* to *Escaret*	1
From *Escaret* to *Zubiri*	1
From *Zubiri* to *Verdey*	1
From *Verdey* to *Garsuena*	$\frac{1}{2}$
From *Garsuena* to *Ancholit*	$\frac{1}{2}$
From *Ancholit* to *Irot*	$\frac{1}{2}$
From *Irot* to *Zabaldica*	1
From *Zabaldica* to *Ugarte*	$\frac{1}{2}$
From *Ugarte* to *Villalva*	1
From *Villalva* to PAMPLONA	1
Total of leagues from *Bayonne* to *Pamplona*	23

Many parts of this last road are very bad. Between *San Juan Pie de Puerto* and *Roncesvalles* there is a frightful declivity on the French side of a mountain, which cannot be descended in a coach, without the assistance of four pair of oxen; that is, one pair to lead the coach, and the other three to hold it up behind, that it may go down slowly.

The country about *Roncesvalles* and *San Juan* is rocky for many leagues on all sides:

fides: yet no tract in Europe has been taken more notice of in ancient romances and poems, nor any battle fo often defcribed, as that of *Roncefvalles,* in which *Orlando* and all the *Peers of France* loft their lives. In the fmall church of the poor village of *Roncefvalles* the brave *Orlando*'s remains were buried, and part of his armour or weapons preferved during many ages. The people of the country tell you fo.

The ROAD
From *Bayonne* to *Vittoria*.

	No. of leagues
From BAYONNE to the river *Bidaffoa*, called *Beovia* by the Spaniards	6
From that river to *Irun*	½
From *Irun* to SAN SEBASTIAN	1½
From SAN SEBASTIAN to *Urnieta*	1
From *Urnieta* to *Anduaein*	2
From *Anduaein* to *Villabona*	1
From *Villabona* to *Irure*	½
From *Irure* to *Tolofa*	1
From *Tolofa* to *Alégria*	½
From *Alégria* to *Caftarieta*	½
Carried over	14½

	No. of leagues
Brought over	$14\frac{1}{2}$
From *Caftarieta* to *Legorrieta*	$\frac{1}{2}$
From *Legorrieta* to *Villafranca*	1
From *Villafranca* to *Segura*	2
From *Segura* to *Segama*	1
From *Segama* to *Galarreta*	3
From *Galarreta* to *Luzurriaga*	$\frac{1}{2}$
From *Luzurriaga* to *Heredia*	1
From *Heredia* to *Audicana*	$\frac{1}{2}$
From *Audicana* to *Arbului*	$1\frac{1}{2}$
From *Arbului* to *La Raza*	$\frac{1}{2}$
From *La Raza* to *Lorriaga*	$\frac{1}{2}$
From *Lorriaga* to VITTORIA	1
Total of leagues from *Bayonne* to *Vittoria*	$27\frac{1}{2}$

At Vittoria you are quite out of the Pirenees, and may continue your journey to *Madrid* through *La Puebla* and *Miranda de Ebro* to *Ameyugo*, a fmall town which is eight leagues from *Vittoria*. I fhall foon note down the road from *Madrid* to *Ameyugo*, and tell a few particularities of the road itfelf, having gone it myfelf fo late as February 1769. Let me firft give you that from *Bayonne* to *Madrid*, which

which I went in December 1768, taking *Pamplona* in my way, and not *Vittoria*, though I knew before-hand, that, by croffing the Pirenees where I did, I was to meet with greater inconveniencies than by going the other way. But of inconveniencies on a journey I never thought much, and went that *Camino de Herradura* for no better reafon but that few travellers chufe to do fo, and becaufe I imagined that it would afford a defcription not to be found in any book.

The ROAD
From *Bayonne* to *Pamplona*.

	No. of leagues
From BAYONNE to *Oftaríz*	2
From *Oftaríz* to *Añoá*	2
From *Añoá* to *Maya*	2
From *Maya* to *Berroeta*	2
From *Berroeta* to *Lanz*	2
From *Lanz* to *Ortiz*	2
From *Ortiz* to PAMPLONA	2
Total of leagues from *Bayonne* to *Pamplona*	14

I was,

I was four days in going the above fourteen leagues, and found the road bad enough in several places to frighten any timorous person. But the devil is not so black as he is painted, and I went through it as through a garden. A *Bayonne* I met with a company of three gentlemen and two ladies who were going to *Pamplona* that same way, and joined with them; but made an agreement before we set out, that the first of us who should utter the least complaint against the road, the weather, or the accommodations, should defray the whole company during the remainder of the journey. This whimsical bargain kept us all very chearful, as, instead of complaining, we were all solicitous to praise most what was most offensive. Thus the wind that troubled us on the highest tops, we termed a gentle breeze; called the snowy weather sun-shine; fed upon imaginary capons, green-peas, and pine-apples, and slept upon seven silk

matrasses

matraſſes like ſo many Spaniſh queens, though our beds were as hard as rocks.

We left *Bayonne* at noon, and went to ſleep at *Añoá*. The road was called excellent during thoſe four leagues, eſpecially wherever we waded through a deep mire, as we did in ſeveral places. However, the country throughout was moſt romantically beautiful, and numberleſs trees ſtill preſerved their verdure in ſpight of the advanced ſeaſon. The poſada at *Añoá* proved much better than I expected, as we found there an ample ſupper and clean beds, and the evening was beguiled with aſking the names of various things in the *Baſque Language* of the people in the poſada. I will here note down a few for the ſake of the Linguiſt that may happen to read this account.

God, Ghinquá.
Man, Ghiſſoná.
Woman, Emaſtaquiá.

Yes,

Yes, sir, Bai yauna.
No, sir, Es yauna.
Yes, madam, Bai andriá
No, madam, Es andriá.
The Sun, Igosquía.
The Moon, Ilarguía
The Stars, Issarac.
A House, Achié.
A Dog, Sciaccourá.
A Cat, Catoúya.
A Rat, Arrotoúina.
A Horse, Sammariá.
A Mule, Mandoá.
An Ass, Astoá.
An Ox, Illiá.
A Cow, Behiá.
A Sheep, Scicchirroá.
A Hog, Scerriá.
A Wolf, Otscioá.
Bread, Oghiá.
Wine, Arnoá.
Meat, Arraghiá.
Fish, Arraína.
The head, Borrouva.

The

The nose, Sudurra.
The mouth, Ahóa.
The tongue, Mihía.
The hand, Efcouva.
A Boy, Mutíla.
A Girl, Nefcáchia.
Fire, Shouva.
Water, Aurá *or* Urá.
Air, Airía.
Earth, Loura *or* Lura.
The Sky or *Heaven,* Serrúa.
Father, Aitá.
Mother, Ama.
Son, Seméa.
Daughter, Alavá.
Uncle, Offáva.
Aunt, Izeba.
Coufin, } Iloba.
Nephew,
A Maid-Servant, Neleatoá.
A married Man, Ghiffoná efcondoá.
A married Woman, Andriá efcondoá.

Whoever

Whoever is poffeffed of Laramendi's *Dictionary of the Bifcayan language*, may by means of thefe few words give a guefs as to the difference between the *Bifcayan* and *Bafque*.

On the fecond day we dined at *Maya*, having in the morning left behind us the fmall town or village of *Ordac*, which is the firft place in Spain. The firft thing that ftruck me on entering the Spanifh dominions was a noble convent that contains twenty two monks. The good fathers have more than fufficient revenues in the neighbourhood; yet, as I was told, have found means to procure the hatred of every body round them, becaufe they have of late ftarted many pretenfions to fome lands, that have long been reckoned as commons.

At *Maya* we dined round a fire, that was lighted in the midft of a fmall room. The fmoke was very troublefome; but in confequence of our agreement we called it a perfume. The pofadero gave us us fowls newly killed, some pork that was eatable, some salt-fish, cheese, and roasted chesnuts, and made us only pay *fifteen sous* a piece. The bread was coarse, but savoury, and the wine would have been excellent if it had been a few months older.

Before sun-set we reached *Berroeta*, where we had a supper plentiful enough, but horrible rooms and very hard beds. In the morning we had gone up a steep and broken hill during three hours; and we crossed a wide plain in the afternoon that produces much wheat and flax, and is planted in several parts with apple-trees, out of which the inhabitants make a cyder tolerably good. That ascent in the morning we found planted on every side with trees of various kinds, especially oaks and chesnut-trees. There was nobody at *Berroeta* that could understand Spanish, except a little sprightly girl. She obliged us with several *Basque*-songs, the airs of which I did not dislike.

There

There I bought of a peasant *The Imitation of Christ*, translated into Biscayan from the Latin of *A Kempis* by a priest of *St. Jean de Luz* called *Abbot Chouno*. That abbot died not long ago, and left behind so good a name, that he goes now by the appellation of *the Saint*. The people at *Berroeta* assure you very seriously, that, when he died, all the bells at *St. Jean de Luz* rang miraculously of themselves.

They burn at *Berroeta* great quantities of the stalks of Turkey-corn, which shows that they have much of that grain. They make bread with the flower of it, besides a kind of hasty pudding, like the Italian *polenta*. With the leaves of that plant they fill the bags under the bed-matrasses; and as those leaves are in a manner elastick, they take off some part of the haroness of the matrasses themselves, which are filled with tow instead of down or wool. You can scarcely have any conception of the clum-

clumsiness of their house-furniture. Their tables are nothing else but an ill-hewn and thick oaken board supported by four poles, and their chairs may be called an abridgment of their tables. A large and ill-made image, which they term a *Nuestra Señora,* is commonly the chief ornament of every bed-room. Their spoons and forks are made of box-wood, like those of our Capuchin-friars, and you may be sure that the handles of their knives are not of silver. The use of a pair of bellows is unknown, at the posadas at least; and the women fan the fire with their aprons in a very dexterous manner. Candles at *Berroeta* they had none, but made use of copper-lamps filled with a kind of train-oil, as they do in Lapland.

As we rose from our beds in the morning of the third day, we saw that it had snowed the whole night: yet we set out about seven, and successively ascended several high hills during two hours

hours, leaving to the mules the care of finding the road, which the snow did not permit us to see. Between nine and ten we found ourselves on a stony plain, about half a league over, as far as I could judge. The crossing of it proved quite distressful, as the wind blew so cold and violent, that it stopped the mules from time to time. However, we crossed it happily in about an hour, with our faces wrapped up in our handkerchiefs, and reached the opposite declivity without having been blown several leagues off, as we all expected. Another hour brought us to *Lanz*, half frozen. I never went two such bad leagues in my life, and thought it impossible for our two ladies to see the end of them without complaining: yet they bore it out as stoutly as the best of us, and cried to us several times, that that plain was *El jardin de los Pireneos*, " the garden of the Pirenees."

At *Lanz* we had but a very indifferent dinner. It only confifted of fome *Abadejo*, or *falt fifh*, ftewed in oil: but we devoured it greedily, as the air had given us all a moft ravenous appetite. We went two leagues further in the afternoon, croffing a foreft planted with the largeft oaks that I have as yet feen any where. The king of Spain might have a very fine navy out of that foreft, if it was not for the many high hills between it and the fea. We reached *Ortiz* at night, found the pofada very good upon comparing it with the three preceding, had a plentiful fupper, and tolerable beds. Some of the people at that pofada could fpeak a little Caftilian, efpecially the pofadera's three daughters, very tall and handfome girls, extremely courteous and willing to oblige their guefts. We were all in love with them, and they with us, and we paffed a good part of the night chatting, finging, and drinking.

The

The territory of *Ortiz*, which reaches a league round, was all green, and the air there quite as mild and temperate as in England in the best spring-days. 'Tis astonishing how the climate changed for the better in a few hours.

The fourth day we went but two leagues in the morning and reached *Pamplona* by dinner-time. The romantick beauty of those two leagues is not to be described. The road, which runs through the bottom of successive valleys, was bordered on each side by hedges of myrtle during the best part. Several rills moisten those vallies, and give them all that is produced by the greatest fertility. Not far from *Ortiz* begins a river, which has an artificial canal by its side, the water of which is diverted to distant fields and meadows, and the country is filled all round with habitations.

Thus did I cross the Pirenean mountains on that side of Spain. The lodgings along them are generally fuch as any fqueamifh perfon will loath: yet for my part I wondered they were not worfe, confidering that almoft no traveller of any note ever goes that road, but only fome poor muleteers, who care little for the elegancies of life, eat any thing, and fleep any where. However I took notice in fome of the villages of fome houfes that appeared neatly built, with green fhutters on the outfide of their windows; nor do the inhabitants commonly content themfelves with rags, but wear very clean clothes, the men wrapping themfelves up in ample dark cloaks as they walk about, and the women having fine filk handkerchiefs on their necks, with narrow fleeves clofe to the wrift, their double treffes falling down their fhoulders interwoven with large ribbands of various colours. You may eafily imagine that the inhabitants throughout that tract are very ignorant, as they live in a manner feparated from the reft of the world,

world, neither underſtanding, nor being underſtood by the few people that happen to croſs their country from time to time, becauſe of their language. Yet they want neither ſprightlineſs nor good humour, as far as I could judge by the eye. They ſeem to enjoy life contentedly enough, and quite as well as thoſe who are poſſeſſed of all its bleſſings.

My travelling company dropped me at *Pamplona*, where I hired a chaiſe for *Madrid*.

The ROAD
From *Pamplona* to *Madrid*.

	No. of leagues
From PAMPLONA to *Venta Vieja*	1
From *Venta Vieja* to *Venta del Piojo*	2
From *Venta del Piojo* to *Mendivil*	1
From *Mendivil* to *Baraſuaein*	1
A river croſſed over a bridge.	
From *Baraſuaein* to TAFALLA	1
From TAFALLA to *Venta del Morillete*	3
A river croſſed over a bridge.	
From *Venta del Morillete* to *Caparroſo*	1
Carried over	10

	No. of leagues
Brought over	10
From *Caparroso* to *Baltierra*	3
The river Ebro crossed in a boat.	
From *Baltierra* to *Venta de Castejon*	1
From *Venta de Castejon* to *Cintruénigo*	3
Not far from Cintruénigo *the kingdom of* Navarre *ends, and that of* Old-Castile *begins.*	
From *Cintruénigo* to *Venta del Postacillo*	2
From *Venta del Postacillo* to A'GREDA	2
From A'GREDA to *Hinojosa*	3
From *Hinojosa* to *Almenár*	2
From *Almenár* to *Tapuela*	$\frac{1}{2}$
From *Tapuela* to *Zamarcon*	$\frac{1}{2}$
From *Zamarcon* to *Almaray*	2
From *Almaray* to *Almanzan*	2
From *Almanzan* to *Almantiga*	$1\frac{1}{2}$
From *Almantiga* to *Cobertolada*	1
From *Cobertolada* to *Villasayas*	$1\frac{1}{2}$
From *Villasayas* to *Barahona*	$1\frac{1}{2}$
From *Barahona* to *Paredes*	$1\frac{1}{2}$
From *Paredes* to *Venta de Rio Frio*	3
From *Venta de Rio Frio* to *Rio Frio*	$\frac{1}{2}$
Here we enter New Castile.	
From *Rio Frio* to *Rebollosa*	$\frac{1}{2}$
A river crossed over a bridge.	
From *Rebollosa* to *Jirueque*	$2\frac{1}{2}$
From *Jirueque* to *Jadraque*	$\frac{1}{2}$
Carried over	45

	No. of leagues
Brought over	45
From *Jadraque* to *Cafas de Galindo*	$\frac{1}{2}$
From *Cafas de Galindo* to *Padilla*	$\frac{1}{2}$
From *Padilla* to *Hita*	$\frac{1}{2}$
From *Hita* to *Sopetran*	$\frac{1}{2}$

The above river croffed again in a ferry-boat.

From *Sopetran* to *Heras*	1
From *Heras* to *Hontanar*	1
From *Hontanar* to *Marchamalo*	1
From *Marchamalo* to *Aloera*	$\frac{1}{2}$
From *Aloera* to *Azuqueca*	$\frac{1}{2}$
From *Azuqueca* to *Venta de Meco*	2
From *Venta de Meco* to ALCALA' *de Henares*	1
From ALCALA' to MADRID.	6
Total of leagues from *Pamplona* to *Madrid*	60

Some account of the above road.

Pamplona, or *Pampeluna*, though but a small town, has a citadel, a square, and some public walks, that deserve the notice of a traveller. The cathedral of it is Gothick, and has its front oddly ornamented with the representation of cats, pigs, monkeys, and other animals, thrown into various burlesque attitudes. The

The fight of that front called back to my mind the church of the Benedictine monks at *Bourdeaux*, which was built, as they pretend, by Henry II of England when the Englifh poffeffed Guyenne. That church has three gates; and the arches over the two lateral ones exhibit many fmall naked figures of men and women placed in fuch poftures, as it is not fit to tell. The Gothick architects had often very whimfical ideas, as I have obferved in many parts. The number of inhabitants at *Pamplona* amounts to no more than feven thoufand, though it is the capital of a kingdom, the title of which is thought worth wearing by two of the greateft monarchs in the world.

December 16, 1768.

I left *Pamplona* about noon, and went to *Tafalla* to fleep.

When Navarre had its own kings, and before it belonged to Spain, *Tafalla* was a town of fome note, and had a univerfity. At prefent it contains nothing

thing remarkable, that I could see but a *posada*, which is one of the best I have found in Spain. The Biscayan language ceases entirely there, and the Spanish begins. Both at *Pamplona* and *Tafalla* I was somewhat troubled by the flies. You may judge of the mildness of the climate by such a circumstance at such a time of the year. The country between the two towns is chiefly sowed with corn, and is flat throughout. The high mountains that surround that plain on all sides, offer a coup-d'oeuil very magnificent.

December 17.

Dined at *Caparroso*, and supped at *Baltierra*, or *Voltierra*.

The road in the morning ran through a barren plain, and through a fertile one in the afternoon. Both at *Baltierra* and *Caparroso* they burn great quantities of rosemary by way of fuel, which perfumes their kitchens sweetly, and an ass-load of it costs but a *real*, or three-
pence

pence English. I asked a handsome young woman at *Caparroso* whether she was married, and was answered in the negative. Don't you wish to be married, replied a by-stander. *El deſſeo no falta,* said she sternly, *mas los hombres buenos faltan.* "Desire is not wanting; but "good men are wanting." I liked the precision of the expression, and took it down in my memorandum-book.

Caparroso is a place famous throughout Spain for a breed of *Perdigueros,* or *Setting-dogs,* that are reckoned the best in the kingdom.

December 18.

I went in the morning along a desart that produces nothing but thyme, and here and there a plant of rosemary; crossed the river *Ebro* in a boat; dined at *Cintruénigo,* and supped at the *Venta del Portacillo,* or *de Cervera,* as others call it.

Cintruénigo, a village in a very rural situation, is surrounded with fine vineyards

yards and olive-groves. I never faw fuch fine olive-trees any where, and had no idea of their ever growing fo large and high, as they do in that neighbourhood. Walking about while dinner was making ready, I faw many men on thofe trees ftriking down the olives, that were gathered beneath by women and children in wicker-bafkets, and fucceffively carried home.

The olives there, when full ripe, are of a bluifh colour, and emit a fine crimfon-coloured liquor when gently fqueezed. I tried that liquor with the tip of the tongue. It has an offenfive tafte, and a naufeous fmell, together with a cauftical quality, that would foon raife a blifter on the rougheft fkin. 'Tis furprifing how fuch a matter can turn fweet and inoffenfive, when flowing from under a prefs after a fhort fermentation.

At dinner I had fome excellent mutton, an omelet fauced with oil inftead of butter, and some purple-grapes as good as fresh, the grains of which were of a size uncommonly large. In the room where I dined, there was a wooden St. Francis, or St. Anthony, as big as the life, with a wooden child in his arms, not quite a span in length. The disproportion was absurd; but the women of the posada seemed not aware of it, and courtesied to it with great reverence every time they crossed the room, and the men pulled off their hats and bowed.

The *Venta del Portacillo* is the very worst lodging that ever I was in. Travellers must take care to avoid it, if possible, especially at night, because the few rooms in it are so loathsome, as I would not permit my dog to sleep in them. 'Tis not necessary to tell what makes them loathsome. There I passed the night sitting and dozing in my chaise in company with my calessero, who has a right to sleep in it every night, and

chuses

chufes to do fo, rather than lie on the bare ground in the ftables, as the muleteers generally do, wrapped up in the coverings of their mules. The fupper that was offered me there, was of a piece with the lodging, as it confifted of fome chopped goat-flefh, fried in an iron-pan with fome rank bacon, the ftrange mefs highly feafoned with garlick, onions, and pepper. A delicate ragout, I affure you; and yet a band of muleteers fell upon it very bravely. For my part I foaked fome bread in chocolate, and called it an evening breakfaft.

That venta ftands alone in a bottom of a rocky valley. I beguiled the evening chatting with thofe muleteers by the fire-fide in a dark kitchen on the ground-floor, that was paved with pebbles of various fizes. No frolickfome coquettifh girls there, as in many other parts of *Navarre*, and in the *Païs de Basque*. Only two ugly women, both out of humour with their hufbands, with their guests, with their cats, and with themselves. I was glad when the morning appeared.

The whole road from *Pamplona* to *Venta del Portacillo*, is as broad and as fine as any in France. The brave General Gages, late viceroy of Navarre, had it made a few years ago. He intended to have all the roads throughout his government enlarged and repaired: but death hindered the laudable scheme from having its effect. He forced the peasants to work at that road by turns, as they do in France; but, to keep them from grumbling, distributed so much of his money to them, that he beggared himself, and died quite poor. A noble monument was erected to him at the public expence in a church at *Pamplona*. 'Tis pity that all the viceroys, and governors of provinces throughout Spain, are not actuated by the same noble spirit.

December

December 19.

Dined at *A'greda,* and supped at *Hinojosa.*

From the *Venta del Portacillo* to *A'greda,* the road was stony, and very bad, and still worse from *A'greda* to *Hinojosa,* up a steep hill, that goes by the name of *Monte Madero.* I had another hill in sight the whole day, that is called *La Sierra de Mayo,* whose elevated top is covered with everlasting snow, like the highest summits in the Alps.

A'greda is an ugly town built on the side of an eminence. I never saw streets so ill-paved and inconvenient: but its territory looks fertile, and offers many romantick prospects. The inhabitants bear great devotion to a female saint, called *Mary of A'greda,* of whom they tell too many idle and absurd stories. 'Tis strange how *Padre Fray Ximenes de Samaniego* could venture upon the tales he has invented, to honour that countrywoman of his, in the life that he has

written

written of her. I never read a more ridiculous book, which is alone sufficient to warrant the French proverb levelled at great liars: *Il eſt menteur comme la Vie d'un Saint.*

The walls of the rooms in the poſada at *A'greda*, are chalked with much verſe and proſe. I ran with my eye over part of it, and never ſaw ſuch a medley of nonſenſical piety and nonſenſical ribaldry.

Travellers are obliged at *A'greda* to go to a public office to procure a *Guia*, or *Paſſport*, for themſelves and their baggage. Such *Guias* are granted *gratis*; and the gentleman who gave me mine, uſed me with great civility, after having quitted his dinner to write it out.

Hinojoſa is a poor village built on the ſummit of a hill. The people at the poſada treated me kindly, and did their beſt to accommodate me at night, filling a mattraſs on purpoſe with new ſtraw. They all wondered at my writing with a *pluma de palo ſin tinta,* " *a wooden pen without*

"*without ink;*" so they termed my pencil; and the good-natured posaders seemed much affected at my ... in presenting him ... with one, after having taught him to sharpen it. None of them had any idea of it, and all inspected it very attentively, to my no small diversion. In several other parts of Spain, and in the *País de Basque* I found also many people that wondered at the uncommon ingenuity of such a thing as a pencil.

December 20.

Dined at *Almaray*, and supped at *Almazán*.

From *Hinojosa* to *Almaray* the country abounds with springs to such a degree, that they render the road almost impassable; and it was by an unremitted continuation of efforts, that the mules dragged the chaise out of the numerous bogs. Both at *Almaray* and at *Almazán* the posadas are very bad. Bad bread, bad

bad wine, bad victuals, bad rooms, and bad beds.

December 21.

Dined at *Barahona,* commonly pronounced *Barauna,* and supped at *Rio Frio.*

Barahona has got the whimsical appellation of *Lugar de Brujas,* " *The witches' town.*" When you read in a Spanish play of a *Barahona-woman,* remember that it means *an* old witch, *an old hag, an old sorceress.* 'Tis one of the standing jests of the Spanish nation, of which I have not yet been able to trace the origin. *Doctor* Aldrete in his Spanish Etymologies only says, under the word BARAHONA, that *en este campo ay fama de juntarse los brujos y las brujas a sus abominaciones, llevados por ministerio de el demonio:* " In this territory, they say, " witches of either sex join to carry on " their abominacions, assisted by the devil." To these words he adds with a gravity

very

very neceffary in Spain, *Es hablilla, y-no ay que darle credito,* " 'Tis a fable that " muft not be credited."

Though the fun shone very bright without doors, yet we could not fee each other in the kitchen at the pofada, becaufe it has been fo contrived that it has no other light, except what comes in at a fmall hole in the cieling, through which the fmoke of the chimney finds its way out with much difficulty. By the fire of that kitchen I dined with a Spanifh officer upon fome hard eggs and *pimentón,* or *pickled Spanifh-pepper*. The officer revenged himfelf of the meagre fare by plaguing the old pofadera with a thoufand jefts on the old women of the place, and made her fo angry that fhe loaded him with the groffeft abufe, to the no fmall diverfion of fome foldiers he had with him, who laughed very heartily. I never heard a more comical dialogue.

My supper at *Rio Frio* was little better than my dinner at *Barahona*; but I had a merry dance by the table at which I ate, and that made the evening agreeable enough. I slept at night in a room without windows, and in a very short bed, which was worse. The Castilians, as well as the Navarrans, are in general pretty tall; yet both in Navarre and Castile the beds are so short, that a man of ordinary size cannot lie extended.

As I was coming along in the morning I met with three men who were going a-foot to *Madrid*. I walked a while with them after having granted them the permission of putting their *capas* or *cloaks,* in my chaise, which proved troublesome in walking. Besides his *capa* one of them put also down his hat; but placed it so carelessly, that it dropped unperceived and was lost. *Alabado sea el Santissimo,* *(praise to the most Holy)* said the poor fellow the moment he was aware of his

misfor-

misfortune: and spoke the words so feelingly, and gave such a look of resignation, that it went to my very heart. Upon such an occasion an Englishman would have uttered an oath rather than an ejaculation: but the Spaniards are far from being so addicted to swearing and cursing as the English. Sudden recollection, and humble patience in adversities that cannot be helped, are virtues, as far as I have observed, much oftener practised in Spain, than in any other christian country. My calessero in the most difficult passes, seldom or never lost his temper, but exerted himself vigorously in supporting the chaise and encouraging the mules, which he never cursed, but only called them Demonios when he thought that they did not obey him with the promptitude he expected.

December 22.

Dined at *Jadraque* and supped at *Padilla*.

The morning-ride was fix full hours through a mountainous country, fome parts of which were covered with feveral kinds of overgrown trees, and fome cultivated and fowed with wheat. It is obfervable in Spain, that the ploughing hufbandman does not make his furrows fo ftraight and even as they do in England and in Italy. This kind of ruftick negligence prevails much in the cornfields that I have feen to-day.

At *Jadraque* I fent for a barber to put my head a little in order; but he fent me word that he could not come, becaufe the fun was fo fine that it was pity not to enjoy it after the many days of cloudy weather they have had. Did you ever hear of fuch a heliotrope? No man of any other nation would have thought of fuch a reafon for his forbearing to get a penny upon occafion.

Not far from *Padilla* I faw a woman felling apples by the weight. Her
fcales

scales were two small wicker-baskets; the beam a stick; and the baskets hung on packthread. I thought the invention very simple.

December 23.

Dined at *Hontanár*, and supped at *Aloéra*, or *La Louera*; a poor posada at one place, and a poorer at the other. However, at *Aloéra* I was well entertained with some extempore *Siguedillas* by two pretty girls, who would not at parting permit me to kiss them but on the forehead, though one was but ten and the other eleven years old.

December 24.

Crossed *Alcalá de Henarez* before day break; had a decent dinner at *Torrejon de Ardóz*, and reached Madrid in the evening. At the *Puente de Viveros*, on the wall of a small and indifferent house, occupied by a man who receives a small toll from those who cross the *Puente* or *Bridge*, I read this inscription. *Hizo esta obra siendo corregidor de la villa de Madria*

Madrid el Senor Don Alonzo Perez Delgado. That is, " This work was done by " Don Alonzo Perez Delgado while chief- " magistrate at Madrid." I like very well the simplicity of the style in this inscription; but cannot help thinking it somewhat ridiculous, that a chief magistrate should be so eager after fame, as to wish to have his name transmitted to posterity upon the account of so inconsiderable a thing as that toll-man's house.

Thus was my journey from *Bayonne* to *Madrid* happily ended, though performed in the most unfavourable season, through difficult mountains, and across regions, the inhabitants of which are as yet much inferior to other nations with respect to the knowledge of the conveniencies of life. In *Old Castile* especially, that inferiority begins at the art of building, which, amongst the indispensable arts, must be considered as the most indispensable. The entrance into an Old Castilian's house is commonly through

through his stable, which, as you may easily imagine, causes a dirtiness in every part of it, that it is not possible to remove. Few houses have more than one story over the ground-floor, and it is not uncommon to find two or three rooms in one house, that have no windows at all, and receive only a little light, either from the door, or from a hole opened in the cieling. The inner-side of their walls differs not from the outside, having no kind of inner covering of plaister, boards, paper, or any thing else; and their floors are no better than their walls, consisting only of a layer of bricks, sometimes of pebbles, kept together by a mortar so ill-composed, that it crumbles soon into dust, and leaves the bricks and pebbles loose; which is also the case with regard to their staircases, that in general seem to have been contrived on purpose to dislocate the climbers' neck, as their steps are made unequal, some high and some low; so that

that you muſt be careful how you go up and down. And yet, many of thoſe houſes, poorly built as they are, have their front decorated with the arms of the owner, carved in ſtone, and fixed over the gate or door.

Under-ground cellars are not much in faſhion throughout *Old Caſtile*, and I ſaw no fire-place in any houſe, but that which belonged to the kitchen. At that fire-place every traveller muſt ſit in winter with the poſadero's family, and almoſt always with a croud of muleteers, aſs-drivers, and ruſticks of all generations, every man ſmoaking his *Cigarro*; that is, a little tobacco wrapped up in a paper, which ſerves him inſtead of a pipe.

At the poſadas you muſt often eat your dinner and your ſupper upon no other table than your own knees, or ſitting aſtride on a bench; and you may well think, that people who want tables and chairs, want alſo many other pieces of houſe-furniture, eſpecially table-linen,

and

and bed-linen, and that what little furniture they have is far from being fine or skilfully contrived. To the use of a candlestick and candles they are utter strangers almost every where; and their common lights are a kind of iron-cups filled with bad oil or other greasy matter, which they hang, by a short iron-handle or chain, to a nail under the chimney, or place on a stool, or on the ground, just as it happens; and I have already said, that in many places they have neither spoons nor forks, but what are made of box-wood. The doors of their rooms (some of which have no door at all) seem generally to have been contrived without the assistance of the carpenter or the locksmith; so that there is scarcely one but what may easily be forced open with a light push. But the security of a good door and a strong lock, is not much wanted in a country, in which there is but little worth stealing, and where, of course, people are not in

the

the habit of appropriating to themselves what belongs to others. It will nevertheless be always prudent in a traveller, to take care of what he has, and not put temptations in the way of people; especially as the posadero's are not answerable in any part of Spain for any thing, that happens to be stolen from strangers.

The men's dress from *Pamplona* to *Madrid*, is the common European, a coat, waistcoat, and breeches; but over it, the *Old Castilians* and *Navarrans*, like most other Spaniards, wear the *Capa*, which I have already described; nor does the habit of their women differ from that which is used in the other Spanish provinces, except that their petticoats are generally green.

Both the *Navarrans* and *Old Castilians* are a tall breed, and seem in general to be very robust. The greatest part have lively black eyes, and the best noses that can be seen; nor is their complexion so tawny

tawny as that of the *New Caſtilians* and *Eſtremadurans*.

On your alighting at a poſada you are ſcarce welcomed by any body belonging to it, nor does any body there take the leaſt notice of you until you call for ſomething. By this kind of neglect, proud travellers are apt to be provoked; and they will fret, and talk big, and make others uneaſy as well as themſelves by ſtorming and ſcolding. But what is cuſtomary cannot eaſily be helped, and all nations have their peculiar ways. The Spaniards ſeem to think, that there is no need to offer their ſervices until they are called upon. Let me therefore recommend the uſeful method of keeping quiet, and of talking and acting with civility and chearfulneſs. By ſticking to it myſelf, I always brought maſters and ſervants about me in a few minutes, and ſeldom had reaſon to blame them for rudeneſs or want of attention. Sufficient experience has taught me, that people of that clafs are eafily rendered kind and officious, and that a ftranger may foon have as many attendants at his beck, as there are perfons in a pofada, the rougheft muleteers not excepted; with whom by the by, I never hefitated a moment to eat and drink, and exchange repartees if occafion offered; and always was the better for fo doing, as otherwife I fhould have often been obliged to keep in a corner by myfelf, and have no body to talk to. The muleteers in Spain are not the fmalleft part of the nation, and I have been affured that there are many of them who poffefs confiderable riches. You meet with large gangs of them on every road, and hear them at a diftance by means of the *Cencerro*, which is an odd kind of large bell, hung by the fide of one of the mules whenever there is a number. Let me now come to fpeak a little of Madrid.

The

The entrance by the Alcalà-gate into Madrid, offers a very noble profpect, as a floping ftreet begins there, which is about half a mile in length, and quite as broad as the broadeft in London, with many good and large houfes and other kinds of edifices on each fide of it. It was a pleafing furprife to me to fee it free from filth, which was far from being the cafe when I firft faw it eight years before.

In Madrid I put up at the *Fontana d'-Oro*, which is reckoned the beft inn in the town: but though I was tolerably well lodged in it, and civilly entertained, yet, as it was my intention to fpend the whole carnival there, I thought fit to remove to a private apartment: and it may not be improper, for the information of travellers, to fay, that at that inn they made me pay at the rate of fix reals a day for the ufe of two rooms, ten reals for my dinner, and eight reals for my fupper. The expence at the private apartment was fomewhat greater; but my rooms were alfo larger, and more decently furnifhed. Adding eight or nine reals a day to a *Valet de Place*, and thirty for the hire of a chariot, the neceffary expence of a foreigner of a private condition will amount in *Madrid* to about four *pefos duros* a day, and I have already faid that a *pefo duro* is equivalent to five fhillings fterling.

During the two months I ftayed in that town, it may eafily be gueffed, that, having once written an account of a former journey through the Spanifh kingdom, I was very bufy in procuring fuch information, as might enable me to rectify that work, and encreafe it in fuch a manner, as to warrant a future publication. With this view I frequented all places of public refort, and endeavoured to the utmoft after the company of the natives, as well as that of the ftrangers who had refided there any time: and fuch was my good luck, that, though my my friend Don Felix d' Abreu was no more, yet I found other friends and acquaintance who in a few days introduced me to a good number of people of various ranks and profeſſions; ſo that, beſides paſſing that ſhort interval to my full ſatisfaction, I had alſo the expected means of correcting ſeveral miſtakes that had ſlipped in the former narrative of my journey, and of augmenting it with a conſiderable number, as I think, of intereſting particularities, by which I hope that my reader will be better enabled to form ſome juſt idea of the Spaniſh nation, than if I had launched into their manners and cuſtoms profeſſedly, as too many travellers before me have dared to do, not much to their honour, in my opinion.

Of the Spaniſh language and Spaniſh literature, I have already ſaid in the foregoing letters whatever I had to ſay. I will only add with regard to the Spaniſh ſtage, that I was not pleaſed ſo much as I expected at the reprefentation of their tragedies and comedies. The practice of their actors in uttering their frequent octofyllables fo deliberately as they do, proved rather difguftful to my ear than otherwife, and made me often wifh that they would go on with fomewhat more of brifknefs and rapidity. However, I muft not attribute my little pleafure to the infufficiency of the actors I happened to hear; much lefs to any intrinfic defect in the Spanifh verfification. The reafon of my difguft muft be my want of being accuftomed to their manner of pronouncing their verfes on the ftage.

I might likewife fay, that their comedians difappointed me with their manner of acting, as much as they did with that of pronunciation; and, to fpeak, my own fenfations, I thought they carried look and gefticulation to extravagance in tragedy, and to caricature in comedy. But this judgment muft like-

wife

wife go for little, if for any thing; and I only record it here as a warning to travelling foreigners not to be so quick as they generally are in their decisions. I have not yet forgot the premature accounts I gave to my Italian friends of the inimitable Garrick on my first arrival in London, for which I have afterwards most miserably blushed many a time. My hasty verdict against him, and some other British actors, keeps me from saying more at present of the Spanish; and were I to pass only a twelvemonth in Madrid, it is more than probable I should be reconciled both to the utterance and action of those, whom Spanish audiences unanimously reckon to be good performers.

The Spaniards have a kind of musical dramas, which they call *Zarzuelas burlescas*. With these dramas I was not only pleased, but thought them much better entertainments than our Italian comic operas. The music of an *Opera Buffa,*

Buffa is perhaps more *learned* (as Frenchmen term it) than that of a *Zarzuela burlesca*; and so far the advantage may be on our side, for aught I know: but on the other hand our dramas of that kind are such detestable rhapsodies of unmeaning nonsense and beastly vulgarity, that no excellence of music can ever compensate the grossness of the composition: whereas in the *Zarzuelas* of the Spaniards, the composer is not at the whole expence of an audience's pleasure, the author endeavours to share the honour of the performance. This at least was the case in one, intitled *Las Segadoras (the Corn-reapers)* exhibited at Madrid in 1768, by *Don Ramón de la Cruz*, and set to musick by *Don Antonio Rodriguez de Hira*. Some scenes of that piece had their full proportion of insipidity, as I thought: but the rusticity of the Spanish peasants was naturally painted throughout; and only the *Cavallero de Madrid* with his affected *Criada* seemed

seemed to depart from truth; nor did the actors think only of their shakes and cadences, as is generally the case with ours; but expressed the words according to their meaning, and with a propriety unknown to the greatest part of ours, who too often mistake grimace for expression, buffoonery for liveliness, and downright meretricious impudence for gracefulness and animation.

The play-houses in Madrid have their peculiarity of disposition like those of England, France, and Italy. These are the parts of a Spanish play-house with regard to the spectators: *El* PATIO, *la* LUNETA, *las* GRADAS, *la* CAZUELA, *la* TERTULIA, *los* APOSENTOS, and *los* ALOSEROS. I must explain you these terms.

El PATIO.

Thus they call *the Pit*, to which no female is admitted. It has no seats, and only the meaner people resort there.

La LUNETA.

'Tis *a Cloſe* betwixt the *Orcheſtra* and the *Patio*, that contains two or three benches for gentlemen only.

Las GR'ADAS.

Theſe are ſome *ranges of ſteps*, which run on the right and left of the *Patio*, amphitheatrically diſpoſed. Gentlemen ſit there as well as in the *Luneta*.

La CAZUELA.

'Tis a kind of *Gallery* that fronts the ſtage, and the place allowed to ôrdinary women. No man is admitted there.

The TERTULIA.

'Tis another *Gallery* over the *Cazuela*. Both the *Cazuela* and the Tertulia have benches riſing gradually backward. The *Tertulia* was once the place where the religious ſat to ſee the *Autos Sacramentales:* but ſince the repreſenting of them was prohibited, it is become a place for any body to ſit in.

Las

Los APOSENTOS.

Thus they call *the Boxes*, of which there are three ranges. The boxes that form the first range (and the second *salvo errore)* are called *Apofentos principales*, and are fuppofed to be occupied by people of rank. Each box is ample enough to contain eight or ten people. A box is commonly hired only for a night, and a company of ladies and gentlemen fit in it promifcuoufly.

Los ALOSEROS.

Thus they call the two corner-boxes on each fide the ftage, and adjoining to the *Gradas.* One of them is appropriated to an *Alcalde de Corte*, or officer of the police, who is prefent at the reprefentation to keep good order. The rank of that perfonage is one of the moft refpectable, and fo high, that the next promotion commonly raifes him to the royal council of Caftile, which is the great council of the ftate.

I have not much to say in commendation of this disposition of a play-house, as it does not offer a very brilliant Coup-d' oeil. Besides that the Spaniards, like the Italians, are too sparing of lights for their pit and boxes, the *Apofentos principales* stand so very high over the *Gradas*, that a man must have very good eyes to distinguish the ladies' faces from any part of the house. Nor must you expect any great satisfaction from looking at the women in the *Cazuela*, who keep their heads covered with their *Mantillas*. Then he who is not used to the sight must be disgusted at the nightcaps, which many a man in the *Tertulia* puts on during the performance, as it is not customary to keep one's hat on in a play-house.

A Spanish audience never makes the least noise before the beginning of the play, as the English do, nor are orange-wenches, or any body else permitted to stun the company with their hideous cries.

cries. The husbands, or the *cortejos*, take upon themselves the trouble of furnishing the ladies in their company with fruit and sweetmeats, of which they have generally a pocket-full, and a servant is commonly kept without, or within the box, that they may send him to fetch *rinfrescos* when they are wanted.

The Spanish ladies, like those of Italy, receive visits in their boxes, and there converse in as loud a tone as they think proper, without fear of being checked by any arrogant voice bidding silence. The Spaniards are too polite, ever to find fault with what the ladies are pleased to do. 'Tis needless to tell, that each division in a Spanish play-house has its particular price. A small part of every play-house-revenue, is appropriated to the maintenance of some hospital.

I wish that to this trifling account, I could join that of the political system pursued in the government of the kingdom. But the shortness of the time I
spent

spent in Spain, and the hurry of the carnival in Madrid, did not permit me to collect so much information as to warrant my launching into such a subject. I can therefore only say, that during the time I was in that town, I heard of no kind of disturbance, public or private; which universal quiet is to be attributed to the several excellent regulations made since the accession of the present king to the throne, and most particularly since the revolt that drove the haughty *Squillace* out of the kingdom. As to the general government of the kingdom itself, I have had it from creditable people, that the king's finances are at present much more economically administered, than they ever were since the days of Philip II; that the navy, though not in a very formidable state, is not at all neglected; and that the army amounts to little less than a hundred thousand men well dressed, well paid, and well disciplined.

To

To provide that army with good artillery-officers and skilful engineers, the king has lately instituted a military school at *Segovia*, to which no *cavallero cadete (young gentleman)* is admitted, who has not, among other, the following qualifications,

1. *Ha de ser Hijodalgo notorio, limpio de sangre y de oficios mecanicos por ambas lineas.*
2. *Ha de saber leer y escribir.*
3. *Ha de ser de buena traza y disposicion personal.*
4. *Ha de ser de doze años cumplidos, hasta quinze no cumplidos.*

In English.

1. "He must be born of a gentleman "publickly known to be such; bear "no consanguinity with Moriscos "nor Jews, and be related to no "mechanicks by father or mother.

2. "He

2. " He muſt be able to read and write.
3. " He muſt have a good look and a " good conſtitution.
4. " He muſt not be younger than " twelve, nor older than fifteen."

The book, out of which I have extracted and abridged theſe ſingular articles, is a ſmall octavo neatly printed, and intitled ORDENANZA *de S. M. para el Real Colegio de Cavalleros Cadetes de Segovia*, MDCCLXVIII. It contains the rules of that inſtitution digeſted under twelve *titulos* or chapters; and will in time be conſidered by Bibliopoliſts as a rare curioſity, as only twelve copies of it have been printed, of which my good luck made me obtain one as a preſent.

I have now ſaid all I had to ſay of Madrid: yet before I quit it the ſecond time, I beg leave to tranſcribe here out of my memorandum-book a few trifles and petty facts, which, collectively taken, may poſſibly aſſiſt more in forming a true

true idea of the Spanish nation, than more elaborate remarks and disquisitions.

A banker's lady told me, that she never masked, nor went to any public ball. Why, madam? *Because,* said she, *I know my own temper, and will not risk the affection I owe my husband.* What would a light Frenchman have replied?

A young gentleman insisted on my placing myself by his sister in her coach, and would forcibly sit backwards. Why do you do so, said I in the usual strain of ceremony. *Because,* said he, *our religion orders us to be respectful to our superiors; and he is always my superior who knows more than I.* I did not expect such a reply from a lad of eighteen, and of the highest quality.

As I was upon my departure from Madrid, a lady asked me which road I intended to take in my return home. Through Old Castile and Biscay, said I. *Do you take Burgos in your way?* Yes, madam, because I want to see that celebrated

brated cathedral. *You ſhall ſee what is ſtill better*, anſwered ſhe. And what is it, madam? *El milagroſiſſimo Chriſto Santo*, replied the lady; meaning a wooden crucifix which is reckoned the moſt miraculous of any crucifix in Spain.

What are you a doing, ſaid I to my landlady as I came to dinner. *I was reciting my roſary while waiting for your coming*, ſaid ſhe.

A ſhoe-maker brought me a pair of ſhoes ſome days later than he had promiſed; and as I reproached him with idleneſs in his buſineſs, he anſwered with great compoſure: *No me falatrá una hora para morir*, " *I ſhall always find time* " *enough to ait*," meaning that it matters little how our time is ſuffered to elapſe, ſince the diligent muſt die as well as the idle.

As a ſervant ſtood looking at a picture, I aſked him whom it repreſented. *Santo Ydelfonzo*, ſaid he. Who was Santo Ydelfonſo? *Chaplain to the Queen of Hea-*

ven. And did he say mass before her, as the king's chaplain before the king? *Who ever doubted that,* replied the man very seriously.

A lady told me, that a Peruvian gentleman just come from his country, wanted to force a piece of money into her hand in her own house by way of token of the pleasure she had given him with a song she had sung; and that he was so affronted at her refusing it, that he quitted her in a pet, telling the company in an angry tone as he was going, that the ladies of *Lima* are as rich as those of *Madrid*, yet have not the rudeness to refuse any pledge of admiration.

It is said, that, when a Spanish lady goes to pay the visit of condolence to her who has lost her husband or other near relation, she is received by the mourner in a room hung with black, and lighted only with one candle. Not a word is spoke by the visiter nor by the visited on such an occasion; but both keep wiping their eyes with their handkerchiefs every other moment for about an hour.

Many authors and editors have the cuftom in Spain to dedicate books to the Almighty, to his Angels, to his Saints, and even to thofe of their images that are in reputation of being miraculous. A volume of Calderon's *Autos Sacramentales* is by a printer dedicated to the *Patriarca San Juan de Dios*, though he was no Patriarch at all, but a bookfeller of *Grenada*, as the dedicatory letter informs us, who in a fit of devotion threw into the fire all the books he had in his fhop, thofe of piety only excepted. That *San Juan* (or *St. John*) was the founder of an order which profeffes ignorance. It was natural for a man who burnt his books, to think of forming fuch an inftitution.

When the edict was publifhed in *Madrid*, that commanded every man to cock up his hat, the whole town was filled with

with murmurs and difcontent. Many a ftranger laughed then, and laughs ftill, at the Spaniards for their not fubmitting with pleafure to a more becoming fafhion: yet we ought to confider how natural it is for mankind to hate innovations, even when they are for the better. Suppofe that the French, or any other European nation, wearing cocked hats, were ordered to uncock them, do you think they would fubmit without reluctance?

I come now to the defcription of the road I took in coming out of Spain the fecond time.

The ROAD

From MADRID to BAYONNE, through *Burgos*, *Bilbao*, and *St. Sebaſtian*.

	No. of leagues
From MADRID to *Alcovendas*	3
From *Alcovendas* to San *Aguſtin*	3
Carried over	6

	No. of leagues
Brought over	6

A river crossed over a bridge.
From San Agustin to the Venta de Pedrezuela	$1\frac{1}{2}$
From that Venta to Cavanillas	$1\frac{1}{2}$
From Cavanillas to La Cabrera	1
From La Cabrera to Lozoyuela	1

A small river waded.
From Lozoyuela to Buytrago	$1\frac{1}{2}$
From Buytrago to Robregordo	$2\frac{1}{2}$
From Robregordo to Somosierra	$\frac{1}{2}$
From Somosierra to the Venta de Juanilla, which is the last place in New Castile.	1
From that Venta to Cerecillo	1
From Cerecillo to Castillejo	1

A small river waded.
From Castillejo to Boceguillas	2
From Boceguillas to Fresnillo de Fuente	$\frac{1}{2}$
From Fresnillo to Carabia	1
From Carabia to Honrubia	2

A river crossed over a bridge.
From Honrubia to La Pardilla	1
From La Pardilla to Milagros	1

A river crossed over a bridge.
From Milagros to Fuentespina	1
From Fuentespina to Aranda de Duero	1

A river crossed over a bridge.
From Aranda to Gumiel de Izam	2

Another river crossed over a bridge.

Carried over	30

	No. of leagues
Brought over	30
From *Gumiel* to *Bahabon*	2
From *Bahabon* to the *Venta del Frayle*	1
From that *Venta* to the *Venta del Junciofo*	1
From the *Venta del Junciofo* to *Lerma*	1
A river croffed over a bridge.	
From *Lerma* to *Villarmazo*	$\frac{1}{2}$
From *Villarmazo* to *Madrigallejo*	$1\frac{1}{2}$
From *Madrigallejo* to *Cogollos*	$1\frac{1}{2}$
From *Cogollos* to *Sarrazin*	1
From *Sarrazin* to BURGOS	$1\frac{1}{2}$
A river croffed over a bridge.	
From BURGOS to *Gamonál*	$\frac{1}{2}$
From *Gamonál* to *Villafría*	$\frac{1}{2}$
From *Villafría* to *Rubena*	1
From *Rubena* to *Quintanapalla*	1
From *Quintanapalla* to the *Monafterio de Rodillas*	1
From the *Monafterio* to *Santa Olalla*	$\frac{1}{2}$
From *Santa Olalla* to *Quintanavides*	$\frac{1}{2}$
From *Quintanavides* to *Caftil de Peones*	$\frac{1}{2}$
From *Caftil de Peones* to *Pradano*	$\frac{1}{2}$
From *Pradano* to *Bribiefca*	1
From *Bribiefca* to the *Venta de Cameno*	$\frac{1}{2}$
From that *Venta* to *Cubo*	2
From *Cubo* to *Santa Maria*	$\frac{1}{2}$
From *Santa Maria* to *Pancorvo*	1
From *Pancorvo* to *Santa Gadéa*	3
Carried over	55

	No. of leagues
Brought over	55

The river Ebro crossed over a bridge called Puente de la Rad.

From *Santa Gadéa* to *Berguenda* - -	1
From *Berguenda* to the *Venta Blanca* -	$\frac{1}{2}$
From the *Venta Blanca* to *Espejo* - -	$\frac{1}{2}$

A River crossed over a Bridge.

From *Espejo* to the *Venta del Monte* - -	$\frac{1}{2}$
From the *Venta del Monte* to *Osma* - -	1
From *Osma* to *Berberaña*, which is the last place in Old Castile - - -	$\frac{1}{2}$
From *Berberaña* to the *Venta de la Peña* -	1
From that *Venta* to *Orduña*, the first town in Biscay - - - -	1

Not far from Orduña you cross over a bridge the Rio de Saracho, by many called Rio de Orduña from the town by which it runs.

From *Orduña* to *Amurrio* - -	1
From *Amurrio* to *Luyando* - -	1
From *Luyando* to *Lodio* - - -	$\frac{1}{2}$
From *Lodio* to *Areta* - - -	$\frac{1}{2}$
From *Areta* to *Miravalles* - - -	$1\frac{1}{2}$
From *Miravalles* to *Arrigoriaga* - - -	1
From *Arrigoriaga* to the *Venta Alta* - -	1
From the *Venta Alta* to BILBAO. - -	$\frac{1}{2}$
From BILBAO to *Gualdacana* - -	$1\frac{1}{2}$
From *Gualdacana* to *Zornosa* - -	$1\frac{1}{2}$
From *Zornosa* to *Durango* - - -	1

| 6 | Carried over | 72 |

	No. of leagues.
Brought over	72
From *Durango* to *Saldivar*	2
From *Saldivar* to *Eybar*	1
From *Eybar* to *Eygobarre*	1
From *Eygobarre* to *Maudara*	1
From *Maudara* to *Zumaya*	1
From *Zumaya* to *Guetaria*	1
A river crossed over a bridge.	
From *Guetaria* to *Saraos* or *Saras*	1
From *Saraos* to *Orrio*	1
Another river crossed in a boat.	
From *Orrio* to *San* SEBASTIAN	1
From *San* SEBASTIAN to *Irun*	$1\frac{1}{2}$
A river crossed in a boat.	
From *Irun* to *Orogne*, which is the first town in France	$1\frac{1}{2}$
From *Orogne* to St. *Jean de Luz*	1
From St. *Jean de Luz* to *Bidars*	2
From *Bridars* to *Bayonne*	2
Total of leagues from *Madrid* to BAYONNE	92

An Account of the above ROAD.

Having been apprised before hand, that many parts of the above road would prove difficult, and absolutely impassable for any wheel-carriage, I thought proper to to hire in Madrid, a couple of mules, one for myſelf, the other for my baggage, of a muleteer who was going to Bilbao with nine more, ſome of which had their loads, and ſome were to have them as they returned from Bilbao to Madrid. The Muleteer, whom I ſoon found to be a very honeſt and hearty man, mounted one of the nine, and his two ſervants, ſometimes riding and ſometimes walking, had an eye upon the whole cavalcade. With them I left Madrid on

February 19, 1769, *in the afternoon.*

We went only as far as *Alcovendas*, a poor village that conſiſts of forty or fifty *Chozas*, as the Spaniards call them; that is, *mean thatched Cottages.* I have already mentioned that village in LETTER LIX. The three leagues from Madrid to Alcovendas afford not a ſpan of cultivated land, and the country is one of the moſt dreary ſpots I have ſeen in Spain.

Though *Alcovendas* is only three leagues from the metropolis, yet the Po-

ſadero

ſadero had nothing to give us for ſupper, except *Bacallao*. But I did not expect better fare, as it was now the beginning of Lent. My ſecond mule not being overloaded, I might eaſily have brought proviſions along, which I could have recruited in all populous places, and have lived upon fowls, hams, and other good things, both morning and evening. But beſides, that by ſo doing, I ſhould have been ſhunned and deteſted as a perverſe infidel, what right had I to ſcandalize any body, and feed highly in the faces of people during a time, in which it is their firm belief, that meager-eating and abſtinence are neceſſary to obtain ſalvation?

At *Alcovendas* we met with two young Biſcayans, who were going to Bilbao like myſelf. They hired one of the nine mules, and agreed between themſelves to ride on it by turns. I liked their thrifty ſcheme, and had reaſon to be pleaſed with them during the journey. One of them was by trade a barber, the other a carpenter. Each was armed with a fire-lock; and it seems that it is a rule with the Biscayans never to travel far without that weapon. By means of kind words, and paying only two or three * *Azumbres* extraordinary every day, I had them both at my disposal during the journey, together with the muleteer and his two men.

My bed at *Alcovendas* was as narrow, short, and hard, as all are throughout Spain in the Posadas. The Posadero's christian name was *Deo Gratias*, and his wife *Conceptionita*, a diminutive of *Conception*. Did you ever hear of such strange names? They put me in mind of *Kyrie* and *Eleyson*, the two formidable knights, whose atchievements are recorded in an old Italian book of chivalry.

February 20.

Dined at the *Venta de Pedrezuela*, and supped at *Lozoyuela*.

This morning, as I was getting upon

---

* *I have already said that an* Azumbre *is a wine measure which contains about a quart.*

my

my mule at *Alcovendas*, the bells of two or three small villages in sight began to ring most noisily. It was a call on the people within hearing, to go and beat the bushes about the neighbouring forest of the *Pardo* for the purpose mentioned in letter LIX.

Having rode about a league from *Alcovendas*, the Biscayans and I entered the forest, as that was our shorter way to *San Agustin*. There we were to rejoin our muleteers, who were taking a larger compass, because no body is permitted to cross it with beasts of burthen. I had seen that forest eight years before, and was not displeased to see it again. A finer one I have never seen. It is chiefly composed of *Encinas*, very properly called *Green Oaks* by the English, as their leaves never lose their verdure. There are millions of them in a space of fourteen or fifteen miles in circumference, and their acorns are more than sufficient to feed its numberless inhabitants.

You know how the writers of chivalry

ry have always been fond of making forests the constant scenes of adventures. It would have been strange if I had crossed so large a one, without meeting with any; therefore I expected at every step, to see some beautiful damsel pop out suddenly from behind a cluster of trees, throw herself down from her milk-white palfrey, kneel before me, and ask me a boon. But as some unkind necromancer would have it, instead of a fair damsel or princess, we met with an ugly fellow, who informed us in a most arrogant tone, that the guns of my two companions were forfeited, as they had contravened the law, which orders that nobody shall carry a gun through a royal forest.

You may well imagine that my poor Biscayans turned pale at the intimation, having nothing to say for themselves. But just as the *Guardia* was going to seize upon their guns, it came into my head that I had my Spanish passport in my pocket, and recollected that it was

expresly

exprefly order'd in it to all his majefty's fubjects to let my worfhip go his way *con fus armas* " *with his arms.*"

What are you doing, cried I to the fellow with the moft imperious tone I could fetch : *How dare you to take away the weapons of my attendants, when this paſſport orders you to let me go unmoleſted with my arms wherever I pleaſe? Read here if you can read, and learn your duty better.*

As good luck would have it, the fellow could fpell with tolerable facility ; and finding that the paſſport was pofitive as to the carrying of *armas* by myſelf or fervants, he abated much of his peremptorinefs, and began to talk in a milder ftrain. To fhorten the ftory, it coft me but a few reals to make him give up his refolution of feeing us before the *Alcalde* at *San Aguſtin,* and turn another way. It feems that the guns would not have become his property in cafe of confifcation ; therefore he was very glad to pock-

et

et a little silver, and quitted us in good humour, after having admonished us to unload them directly, left we should meet with some other *Guardia* more troublesome than himself. Thus ended the adventure, and you may well imagine that the gratitude of the Biscayans proved afterwards proportionate to the service I had done them, and that the barber would never have a farthing for the care he took of my chin during the journey.

By way of dinner at the *Venta de Pedrezuela*, we could only have a couple of *Sardinas* a-piece; and *Pilchard* is the English for *Sardina*. But at *Lozoyuela*, which we reached as the night was far advanced, besides some hard eggs, we had a large omelet seasoned with oil instead of butter, with the addition of a sallad made of raw onions, which my keen appetite made me think the best thing I ever eat.

From the above *Venta* to *Lozoyuela*, the

the country grew mountainous as we went on, but appeared much more fertile than from *Madrid* to the *Venta*. At *Lozoyuela* I slept in my cloaths on a heap of straw, in a room so small, dark, and dirty, that you would have thought it a proper place for a malefactor.

I must not forget, that not far from a village called *La Cabrera*, I saw a gallows by the side of the road, that had a large knife stuck into the cross bar at top; and was informed that the lord of the manor has there a right to hang and quarter any villain, when convicted of having committed a robbery on the highway within his lands. That right which many of the great nobility have in various parts of the two Castiles, is called *El Derecho de Horca y Cuchillo*, " *the right* " *of gallows and knife.*"

From Madrid to *La Cabrera* we had some mountains in view on our left hand, the tops of which were covered with snow. The *Escuriál* is within those mountains,

mountains, thirteen leagues diftant from Madrid. The fnow had fallen this winter fo abundantly about that celebrated place, as to render the road from Madrid almoft impaffable. Adding that reafon to the pleafant life I led in Madrid, I neglected to go and fee it, for which, I own, I am almoft afhamed. To go twice from *London* to *Madrid*, and not ftep to the *Efcurial* is really unpardonable. But I intend to go a third journey on purpofe, if I can ever contrive it.

February 21.

Dined at *Somofierra*, and fupped at *Caftillejo*.

This morning we croffed the town of *Buitrago*, built on an eminence amidft feveral broken hills. Not a century ago *Buitrago* boafted of a noble caftle very well worth a vifit from a traveller. Madam d' Aunoys mentioned it in her *Relation du Voyage d' Efpagne*, and in her ufual ftyle of a novel, defcribed fome pictures

pictures she saw in its apartments. As far as I could judge from without, that poor castle is at present in a declining condition; and if its inner parts are like the outer, there will be an end of it in a little time, which will be a great pity, considering the extreme beauty of its situation, for the country it commands, seems to be quite as fertile as it is romantick.

From *Buitrago* to *Somosierra* through a very stony and difficult road we ascended several hills covered with snow. *Somosierra*, though a very indifferent village, denominates that long chain of high and rugged mountains which divide the *two Castiles*. There we could scarce find any thing to eat, besides bread and onions. While we were at dinner, a young fellow came to us with a dead wolf in his arms, which he laid at my feet. " Behold the beast (said he with " an air of triumph) that shall do you " no harm in your journey through our
" moun-

" mountains. See what a fet of ivory
" teeth! See what terrible jaws and
" fangs! I killed it laft night juft by
" my cot, and he fhall eat no more of
" my kids, *fi el baron San Antonio ferà*
" *fervido*," " *if it pleafes Saint Anthony.*"

I did not diflike the oratory of the man, and treated him as every benefactor to mankind ought to be treated, with much refpect and kindnefs. Though the beaft was none of the largeft, yet the look of it was fufficiently ugly to make one chufe to fee it dead rather than alive. Our Alpine wolves are generally brown, but that was of a dirty kind of white, covered with fhort hair, that ftood ftraight all about the body. When a man is fo lucky as to kill one, his fortune is fomewhat the better for it, becaufe a fum of money (a hundred reals, if I am not miftaken) are paid him by the corporation of his town, befides what is got from private people by fhowing it about, as no body will
refufe

refuse a copper-coin at least, as a reward to his bravery.

Between *Buitrago* and *Somosierra*, at a place called *La Puente de las Fuentes*, there is a stony *cuesta*, or *ascent* so very steep, that it was all our mules could do to mount it without tumbling. A strange *Camino de Ruedas*, thought I: but how any wheel-carriage can be dragged up that pass by any two mules, is what I cannot conceive. I suppose that a chaise is there taken to pieces, as they do at the foot of *Mount Cenis* in Savoy, and carried up disjointed by the peasants in the neighbourhood.

From *Somosierra* to *Castilejo* the road was quite hidden by a snow about a foot thick, which had fallen the night before on some other that was already there. I never went three leagues worse than those, as the road lies across several broken hills, covered all along with large broken stones that lie loose about, and make the mules stumble at every step.

ſtep. 'Tis lucky that a mule has this good quality, that he never falls but on his knees, and, if you will but let him alone, he gets upon his legs preſently. My companions ſtopping at the *Venta de Juanilla* to drink, I was ſo imprudent as to go forwards alone: but had not advanced a mile when my mule pricked up his ears on a ſudden, ſnorted three or four times, and before I was aware of the cauſe of his fear, threw himſelf off the track, down the rocky bank of a ſmall torrent. The bank was ſix or ſeven foot high, and quite perpendicular. I wonder how I kept in the ſaddle, and how he could fall on his four without breaking two or three at leaſt. The jerk he gave in the leap made me ſee a dog at his heels. Full as I was of the idea of the wolf, I thought the dog a wolf, and drew my hanger in an inſtant. The ſun ſhone bright, and the flaſhing of the blade, as I ſuppoſed, frightened him back: but ſeeing me wade along the torrent,

torrent, he returned the fame way and ran ftraight forwards towards *Caftillejo*.

Mean while I was in the torrent, and did not fee how I could regain the road becaufe of the great height and fteepnefs of its banks. I had nothing to do but encourage my mule onwards through the ftream; and fo I did during an hour, with the water up to the mule's knees. At laft I faw a clufter of houfes about half a mile before me, found a place to get out of the torrent, and reached them juft as my company was coming. It was the village of *Cerecillo*, where I faw the rafcally cur that had frightened both my mule and me, and put our necks in no inconfiderable danger, befides puzzling much my muleteer, who could not poffibly conceive what was become of me, as he had not feen the frefh footfteps of my mule for two thirds of a league from *Cerecillo*.

The Road from *Cerecillo* to *Caftillejo* was far from good: but I could fee it, and was glad that we were now quite out of the fnow. 'Tis a moft uncomfortable thing to go along any road that one cannot fee, when it happens to be rugged and difficult. It is true that a mule ufed to it fmells it furely out, be it ever fo narrow, and the fnow ever fo deep: yet that only diminifhes the pain, and one is ftill vexed to travel in that manner, quite at the difcretion of a beaft. We naturally hate to be in their power, be they quadrupeds or bipeds.

I have feen no inconfiderable number of bad villages in many parts of Spain, but *Caftillejo* I thought the worft of them all. The road through it would be a deep bog in winter, if it was not for the many cartloads of large ftones and pebbles thrown along it. Thofe ftones and pebbles are not cemented together, though two or three foot deep. Imagine what a firm footing both mules and men muft find on a road made after that manner. It was worfe than to wade through

the

the torrent. I alighted at the pofada, while the muleteer went a little forward to put up at fome ftables, leaving me and the Bifcayans to fhift for ourfelves. The pofada we found to confift but of one room, befides the fmoaky kitchen. A room, did I fay? It was a nafty hole, that contained two nafty couches, one of which was occupied by a poor old man, who (as I heard afterwards) died that fame night. To take our quarters there was utterly impoffible. What fhall we do, faid I to the honeft Bifcayans. Let us go and fee if we can find a better place for love or money. In the ftreet, or the road, (name it what you pleafe) we met with a prieft, who informed us that there was an old woman in the village, called the *Tia Phelipa (my aunt Philip)* who would give us a good night's lodging, if commanded by the *Alcalde*; otherwife not, as no body can be fo far prejudicial to the pofaderos, as to keep lodging houfes, becaufe the pofadaros pay a tax for keeping theirs; and if travellers were not to go to them on the pretence that their pofadas are bad, the poor rogues would ſtarve, and be ruined. Well then: we went to the *Alcalde*, a well-looking old peafant, who prefently granted my petition, and not only permitted me to go to *Tia Phelipa*, but came himfelf to ſhow me the houfe, and delivered her his orders in perfon that ſhe ſhould treat me well, becaufe I was a *Hidalgo*, faid he, that had a paſſport from the fecretary of ſtate.

The good *Tia*, her fon, and her fon's wife, made us very welcome, and prepared us as good a fupper as was poſſible to have in fuch a place. We cannot faſt to-night, faid I to the *Tia*, becaufe we have had but a very forry dinner at *Somoſierra*. Never fear, faid ſhe; I will give you the beſt fupper you ever ate in your life: and the fupper confiſted in the uſual meſs of *dry beans* boiled in oil, the uſual *bacallao* ſtewed

in

in oil, the usual *sardinas* more salt than brine, the usual *oily omelet*, with only the addition of some *escabeche*; that is, some river-fish pickled with vinegar, sugar, and garlick, together with some *walnuts* and *dry grapes* by way of desert.

Just as we had done eating this Sardanapalian supper, the *Alcalde* returned with the priest, to see how *Tia Phelipa* had treated us. Thank you, thank you, *Senor Alcalde: Tia Phelipa* is the best woman in Castile. But pray, *Señor Cura*, won't you sit down? Here is to you both. Reach them the pitcher, good *Tia. Liquida* * *non frangunt, Señor Cura*, and the weather is very cold. The pitcher, though pretty large, showed its bottom two or three times, and a couple of hours were past very merrily. It was near twelve when they left us. The *Tia*'s beds were clean, and tolerably

---

* *Liquida non frangunt jejunium*; that is, you may drink on a fast-day, though you may not eat.

soft. I had a good night's rest, and forgot the snow, the dog, and the torrent.

February 22.

We dined at *La Honrubia*, and supped at *Aranda de Duero*. I saw nothing extraordinary to-day, but the village of *Fuentespina*, which contains above a hundred houses. At a distance it makes a good appearance, because of the cupolas that many of those houses have by way of roofs; but both the roof and the walls of almost every house are of mud, laid very thick, lest, as I suppose, the rain should wash them away too soon. The territory of *Fuentespina* is almost all taken up with vineyards. *Aranda* is a considerable town, as it contains fourteen or fifteen thousand inhabitants. The *Duero*, by which it is distinguished from another town in Spain of the same name, is a beautiful river; but not navigable.

It was at *Aranda* that I took notice of a custom the muleteers have, of touching

ing a loaf with their right hands as they cross themselves when they say grace after supper. It is the want of holy water that makes them touch the bread in its room. The custom extends to all the lower class of the Spanish people, who have a kind of veneration for bread.

Aranda has belonged to the crown ever since a king of Spain said this rhyme,

Aranda de Duero
Por mi te quiero;

That is, *Aranda by the Duero, I will have thee be mine.* The inhabitants seem proud of their belonging to the king rather than to any other lord. The *posada* at *Aranda* is very bad, though it goes by the pompous name *of the Countess,* "*posada de la Condesa.*"

February 23.

We dined at the *Venta del Frayle,* and supp'd at *Villarmazo*. Nothing but eggs at noon, and eggs again at night.

Coming

Coming out of *Aranda* I saw the land laid out in vineyards during a league. The cheapnefs of wine, both at *Aranda* and *Fuentefpina*, is almoft incredible. With no more than fifty reals in a tolerable year, a family of fix people in each place may buy as much of it as they commonly drink in a twelvemonth; and that is about the quantity of three Englifh hogfheads. Many a man in England will drink that money in an hour.

The *Venta del Frayle*, a wretched houfe, forms about the fixth part of a wretched hamlet, which, together with its territory, belongs to the Benedictine monks. One of the *Padres*, an elderly man, lives in that hamlet as factor to his order, and may without impropriety, be termed *the Pope of the place*, as he exercifes a temporal as well as a fpiritual authority over the inhabitants, whofe number amounts to about forty, women and children included. The petty tyrant obliges them all to hear his own mafs

every

every day, and at the hour he pleafes; will not fuffer them to confefs to any but himfelf; and never would remit any of them a real of their rent ever fince he went to live there, though he knows them to be wretchedly poor. Defpotifm cannot eafily be carried further. I happened to afk what people the good father had at home. No body but a *Calentadór*, anfwered a neighbour flily. A *Calentadór* means a *Warming-pan*; and the title is never beftowed upon old women by the jocular Spaniards.

There are few fpots prettier than that fmall monaftical kingdom. 'Tis a green flat, about a mile over, moiftened by a moft limpid ftream, that defcends from a neighbouring hill quite cover'd with trees. In fummer it muft be delightful to live there.

Reaching *Lerma* by five in the afternoon, and thinking it ftill too early to halt, I chofe to pufh half a league further to *Villarmazo*, though I knew that my company,

company, which I had left behind, intended to pafs the night in *Lerma*. It may poffibly be thought ridiculous, yet I cannot help telling it, that it was with the greateft difficulty I could prevail on my mule to go that half league. The fturdy animal, long accuftomed to ftop at *Lerma* whenever he went that way, forced me to ufe the fpur every moment to keep him a going. He would have ftopp'd at every ftep, turned his head towards *Lerma*, and bray'd with all his might in a moft angry tone. Mules as well as better folks have their habits, which are not eafily to be conquer'd when they are grown too obftinate.

By *Lerma*, which is as confiderable a town as *Aranda*, there is a caftle that travellers go to fee. It is the country feat of a principal grandee, whofe name I have forgot. Almoft all the houfes in the town belong for the moft part to that fame grandee; but few of them are worth much, as they are almoft all built with

wood

wood and mud, like thofe of *Aranda*. The country between the *Venta del Frayle* and *Lerma*, is a defolate heath, through which the road is bad enough, even for mules; and a wheel-carriage in winter, could fcarcely be dragged out of the frequent bogs.

February 24.

We breakfafted at *Cogollos* on a fcanty mefs of *garavanzos* boiled in oil as ufual, and fupped at *Burgos*, the capital of *Old Caftile*.

This was a hard day's journey, though very fhort, becaufe of the execrable road, violent wind, inceffant rain, and a freezing cold, that *matava las manos (killed the hands)* as my Bifcayans phrafed it. About two in the afternoon I reached the miferable village of *Sarazin*, and there was obliged to run for fhelter into a peafant's houfe, becaufe of the rain that poured intolerably faft. The houfe was crouded with people, efpecially women, fitting round a fire that filled the room

with

with a thick fmoke. It diverted me much to fee them all chearfully pinching each other by way of paftime. A fat and grey-headed Dominican friar, who had feen me go by his convent, came after me, and courteoufly brought me a couple of good apples with a bit of excellent bread, which was far from unwelcome. I fent to a neighbouring houfe for wine, made him and the whole company drink repeatedly, and paffed there a couple of hours with much fatisfaction, in fpight of the fmoke, that made my eyes red. It was fix when I entered *Burgos*.

February 25.

We paffed the whole day at *Burgos*. The Welchman *Udal ap Rhys*, in his Account *of the moft remarkable places and curiofities in Spain and Portugal*, calls *Burgos* a *large town*, and fays, that it has *many fine fquares adorned with fountains, many handfome buildings, and fome palaces*. Yet I will be fo bold as to fay, that

that *Burgos* is a small town, very ill built, very dirty, and containing only one square surrounded with wretched houses. Its cathedral and the archiepiscopal palace are the only edifices that deserve attention. They are both Gothick, and both huge enough; the cathedral especially, which contains fourteen or fifteen chapels and a sacristy very grandly adorned. It would require a volume to register the riches that some of those chapels contain. In the middle of the church there is an enclosed sanctuary, made after the manner of the *Holy Chapel* at *Loretto*, which was built long after the church, as one may see by the style of its architecture, which is of the Corinthian order. That sanctuary contains a miraculous crucifix, or *Christo*, as they call it there; yet not quite so miraculous as another that is in the church of the Augustines. In the church of the Trinitarians there is a third, miraculous likewise.

Without

Without the town there are some public walks very pleasant, as they overlook a romantick landscape beautified by the rapid and noisy river *Arlanzòn*, which is crossed over by a stone-bridge very well built.

An industrious Frenchman has just set up a coffee-house with a billiard-table in Burgos. The novelty of the thing attracts much company there, and all the young idlers of the town live in a manner at that coffee-house. To avoid the frequent quarrels that arose at first between them and the Frenchman, the governor, who makes it a point to patronize the new establishment, has lately published an edict, which I will transcribe and translate for its singularity.

TARIFA

TÁRIFA *del precio aque se venderan los generos en el Caffé Francés, y lo que se pagará por cada partida de trucos y villár con approvation de la justicia.*

	Reales.	Maravedis.
Una Taza de cafee de Moka con el azucar que cadauno quisiere, poner, aunque sea con leche - -	1	
Una Taza con leche, ò sin ella	1	
Una Gicara de buen chocolate, con leche, ò sin ella, y con pan correspondiente tostado - -	1	
Un Baso de quartillo de Babaduesa, con Jarave de Capilér, con leche, ò sin ella - -	1	17
Una copa de qualquier licor, ò espiritu de Francia - -	1	
Cada Botella de vino estrangero se pagará segun su calidad		
Una libra de Dulces de Francia	12	
Cada Bollito para tomar chocolate	24	
Si es doble - -	1	14

Vol. IV. U *Una*

	R.	M.
Una Baraja de Naypes para juegos permitidos de noche con luces	4	
Idem, una usada que esté limpia	3	
Idem, una nueva de dia -	3	
Idem, una usada - -	2	17

Quien rompiere Jicara (above it is spelled *Gicara,*) *Taza, Vaso* (above it is spelled *Baso,*) *ú otra cosa, lo pagará por su justo precio. Se jugará hasta las diez de la noche, pues no permite mas el Señor intendente corregidor.*

In English.

" *A Tariff of the prices at which*
" *the things at the French coffee-*
" *house are to be sold, together*
" *with what is to be paid for*
" *every game at billiards, as set-*
" *tled by government.*

" *A dish of Moka-coffee with as*
" *much sugar as any body chuses,*
" *though it be with milk* -   1

" *A dish*

	R.	M.
" A dish of tea, with or without milk - - - -	1	
" A dish of good chocolate, with or without milk, with its due proportion of toasted bread -	1	
A glass of Capillaire, with or without milk - - - .	1	17
Any French dram - -	1	
Each bottle of foreign wine shall be paid for according to its quality.		
A pound of French sweet-meats	12	
A chocolate-cake - -		24
If double - - -	1	14
A new pack of cards to play at lawful games by night and with lights - - -		4
An old pack, but clean -		3
A new pack, by day -		3
An old pack - -	2	17

Whoever shall break a cup, glass, or other thing, shall pay its just price. Playing shall last till ten at night,

night, as the civil magiſtrate forbids the continuation of it beyond that hour.

The reader may take notice, that, by ſome unaccountable overſight, the price to be paid for playing at billiards, has been intirely omitted, though announced in the title of this Tariff.

There are three or four poſadas at *Burgos,* two of which are reckoned good, after the manner of the country. I had a paſſable room and tolerable fare in that where I put up. They call it *La poſada del Marqués.* But the landlady there, is one of the moſt deteſtable old women in Spain. She would beat her little children for nothing ſeveral times a day, and ſcold and curſe every body and every thing, even while ſhe was muttering over her beads. She aſked me during a ſhort interval of good humour whither I was going. To England, ſaid I: *Inglaterra mala Tierra,* anſwered ſhe; that is, " England is a " wicked country." How do you know that,

that, *Señora?* *I know,* she replied, *that they are wicked Hereticks there, that ought all to be drowned.* Why so? *Para que la casta se pierda,* " that the breed " may be lost," replied the ugly wretch. One of her maids, a young woman about twenty, is what they term a *Beáta*; that is a girl who has made a vow never to wear a gown, but what is made of a coarse woollen stuff of an ash-colour. Yet her vow does not interfere with her coarse gallantry, as far as I could guess.

The Mendicant Friars, and even some of those who are not Mendicant, have a custom in several parts of Spain, and at *Burgos* especially, to watch the arrival of strangers at the posadas, in order to put them under contribution, which they effect by asking alms for the sake of a crucifix, a virgin, or some saint, which they produce from under their garments.

Some Pofaderos, who have often had occafion to obferve how much the generality of travellers diflike fuch kind of vifits, will not permit the importunate fathers to enter their doors, but make them wait without, and only give them leave to fend in their images, which are often returned with a mere compliment, a traveller being then more at liberty to refufe the requeft, as the beggar is not prefent, to whofe habit and profeffion it always looks indecent to deny a fmall piece of money. For my part however, I was never much difpleafed at their admiffion; and their ftories of fevers, head-achs, and other diftempers miraculoufly cured by their images, feemed always to me a fufficient equivalent to a *real*. Were you to give credit to what they all fay, there are none of their images but perform an incredible number of *milagros portentofos*: yet afk any Spaniard if he has ever feen a miracle performed; and it is a hundred to one but he anfwers in

the

the negative: but his imagination eafily runs away with him, and he is ftill perfuaded that every image is miraculous, as his mind has been crammed with that notion ever fince the day he was born. Notwithftanding this, I cannot help being of opinion that, fooner or later, the friars will break their bows by overftraining them, and that what has already happened in many countries, will likewife happen in Spain, if meafures are not taken to check their boldnefs in abufing the credulity of the vulgar. I know that the vulgar may be kept long in the fold of fuperftition; but let them watch the enclofure with unremitted vigilance, and take the greateft care that it be no where broken; or they are undone, as they have been in thofe countries which they call heretical. In whatever fubjection they may keep the lower ranks, one of their orders has lately found by woeful experience, that the higher are no longer to be made fools of; and of the lower ranks themfelves I have myfelf feen fome, who looked irreverently at the *Piél del Gran Lagarto*; that is, at the *fkin of an Alligator* ftuffed with ftraw, which the Auguftines have in their church at *Burgos*. The animal, to whom it belonged, at the interceffion of one of their Saints, is faid to have vomited up a man alive, after having kept him in his belly, I know not how many days.

February 26.

I fet out from *Burgos* at eleven in the morning, reached *Quintanapalla* at two, and there dined upon raw leeks and falt; but fupped well at *Caftil de Peónes*, at the houfe of my muleteer who lives there. His two daughters, very tall and comely girls, who had previous intelligence of an *Hidalgo* coming home with their father, gave us a treat, that confifted of fome frefh-water-fifh, an omelet made with butter at my defire, inftead of oil, fome *efcabeche* of their own pickling, and other things. It is not the cuftom
among

among the common people of Spain (as far as I have feen) for daughters to fit with their fathers and brothers at table: yet I infifted upon their giving us their company, which was granted after fome ftruggle, and thus was the evening fpent very agreeably. The propriety of behaviour in women of the lower clafs, has often aftonifhed me in Spain. A great many of them feem to be polite by nature; and my Muleteer's daughters bore their part in the converfation at fupper with a gentlenefs and modefty, that would have captivated a favage. Had I met with them in any houfe at Madrid, I fhould not have found them to be ruftick girls by their manners. The female drefs from *Quintanavides* to *Berberaña,* which is the laft town in *Old Caſtile* on the fide of *Bifcay,* continues to be the old Spanifh drefs, and confifts of a robe, generally brown, that runs clofe to the neck and wrifts, with feveral cuts along the fleeves from the fhoulder to the elbow, and a

'broad

broad girdle buckled round the waift. I think it a drefs very becoming and moſt advantageous to a fine ſhape. They form their long hair into a twift which hangs behind, and cover their heads with a *Montéra*, or black felt-cap, that gives the young people a very ſmart air. The Muleteer's houſe was far from containing any thing elegant; but I did not perceive in it any want of ruſtick conveniencies. His kitchen had a good ſtock of copper-pans, pewter-diſhes, and earthen-plates. His table-linen, though coarſe, was clean, and his beds and bed-coverings of a decent ſize, a thing not common in the Poſadas. He had even two ſilver-ſpoons laid upon the table, and informed me with a true fatherly ſatisfaction, that they belonged to his daughters, who had earned one a piece by their ſpinning. The Surgeon of the place, a well behaved gentleman-like peaſant, ſupped with us, and contributed his ſhare to the general joy of the company, by ſinging ſome ſongs to

the guittar. From him I learnt, that in moſt villages of *Old Caſtile* the firſt perſon is the *Curate*, the ſecond is the *Alcalde*, and the third the *Surgeon*. The income of the laſt of theſe conſiſts of a *Fanéga*, or Buſhel, of corn, from every houſe-keeper; which, on a general computation amounts at *Caſtil de Peones*, to almoſt four *reáls*, or a ſhilling a day. In return for this ſalary, the Surgeon is obliged to ſhave every body that wears a hairy chin, bleed and cup all who want it, and play the phyſician upon ſmall occaſions, though his preſcriptions ſeldom go beyond recommending abſtinence, warm water, and a bed perfumed with roſemary. The *Alcalde*, or Mayor, is choſen by the corporation from amongſt the more ſubſtantial inhabitants, and his office laſts a year. His profits are inconſiderable. The curacy at *Caſtil de Peones* brings no leſs than ſix thouſand *reáls* which makes ſomething more than ſeventy pounds ſterling; an enormous ſum in ſuch a place. I aſked what ſort of
a Curate

a Curate they had, and was anfwer'd much to his honour, and that he diftributes all he can fpare amongft his poorer parifhioners. *Gracias á Dios,* faid the Surgeon, *nueftro buen Cura es baftante Letrado, y tiene mas de cien Libros,* " thank " God, our good Curate is fufficiently " learned, and is poffeffed of above a " hundred books."

February 27.

We dined at *Pancorvo,* and fupped at *Ameyugo.*

There are two roads from *Caftil de Peones* to *Pancorvo,* one of *ruedas* through the town of *Bribiefca,* the other of *herradura* through a dreary common about three leagues in length. This laft is about a league longer than the other; yet we took that, becaufe the former was impaffable, the rain having filled it with mire. Not far from *Caftil* we mounted a difficult afcent, and croffed the common. One of the Bifcayans and I, trotted away to *Pancorvo* and reached it

about

about three in the afternoon, which was a ride of seven long leagues, the three last so very bad, that our mules were often in the mud up to their bellies.

At *Pancorvo* a very civil Posadera gave us a tolerable dinner, and you must have learned by this time what a tolerable dinner means. She would fain have engaged us to stay the night, and I was much inclined to do so, being fatigued with my long ride: but our company overtaking us, the Muleteer insisted on our pushing so far as *Berguenda*, which was four leagues further. This I absolutely refused, my weary limbs not being able to go so far. After a short altercation we agreed to go and sleep at *Ameyugo*, which is but a league and a half from *Pancorvo*. *Ameyugo* was about half a league out of the main road; yet it advanced us a league. It is through *Ameyugo* that the traveller goes, who will cross the Pireneans between *Vittoria* and *Bayonne*; as

from

from *Ameyugo* you go to *Miranda de Ebro*; from *Miranda* to *La Puebla*; from *La Puebla* to *Vittoria*; and so to *Bayonne*, returning by the same road that I have noted p. 198 and 199 of this volume.

We were about three hours in going from *Pancorvo* to *Ameyugo*, as part of the road was covered with a layer of pebbles about two foot deep, and thrown at random upon it, to render it practicable in winter across many sloughs. Those pebbles lying loose, make it impossible for the mules to march along with a steady pace, and their irregular motions fatigue an unaccustomed rider more than one would be apt to imagine.

Not far from Ameyugo we found the highway running through a valley formed by *riscos* and *peñas*, as the Spaniards call them; that is, by naked rocks and cliffs of enormous sizes, many of which are as high as the highest towers. They appeared with a dreadful kind of majesty

on

on each fide the road during half a league, and fome of them hung over it in fuch a manner, as if they were going to fall down upon the paffenger. Should any of them ever break and tumble, it would require the labour of thoufands to clear the paffage from the fragments.

We reached *Ameyugo* two hours after fun-fet, half perifhed with cold; but found fo good a fire at the Pofada, that it foon reftored us the ufe of our limbs. There are large groves of fir-trees amongft the *rifcos* and *peñas* in the neighbourhood, which furnifh the inhabitants with plenty of fuel. A fire made of fir-wood cafts a fmell fomewhat too ftrong; yet not difagreeable. At *Ameyugo* a couple of roafted apples were my fupper, and, being quite tired, went to bed in a room that had not even fhutters to the windows; yet, placing myfelf under a heap of coverings, I flept very comfortably and without interruption till fix the next morning.

February

February 28.

We dined at *Espejo*, and supped at *Orduña*.

In all my travels I never had a day's journey so fatiguing as this, and was sixteen hours on mule-back, though we went but ten leagues. The face of the country from *Ameyugo* to *Espejo* looked delightful, nor was I displeased with the prospect round *Osma*; and so far the road was tolerable. But from *Osma* to *Berberaña* it runs across a ground, that might not improperly be termed *the summit of a mountainous rock cut smooth and aslant*. I wondered how the mules could keep their footing upon a declivity so hard and sloping. Yet the difficulty and danger of going over it was next to nothing when compared to what we met from *Berberaña* to the *Venta de la Peña*, that is, to a lodging house which stands alone on the top of the high *Peña*, or mountain, which divides Old Castile from Biscay. Between *Berberaña* and that *Venta* there

is

is the fide of a hill fucceeded by fuch an uneven plain, as I know not well how to defcribe. The ground is there of fo foft a nature, that it yields and finks under the hoofs of the mules, a few of whom going in a row one after the other, are fufficient to form a deep track; yet fo narrow, that it foon becomes next to an impoffibility for the next mules that pafs that way to keep in it. This natural quality of the ground obliges the muleteers to look about for fome place that has not been newly trodden; and their inceffant varying their courfe down the fide of the hill, and over the plain, has filled both with numberlefs paths, that lie in various directions, interfect each other, and chequer the ground in a ftrange manner.

It is furprifing to fee during a league how the mules ftep fhort every now and then, examining how they fhall advance, and endeavouring to avoid the innumerable ftumbling places along that treacherous ground. Had *Des Cartes* ever travelled that road, he would prefently have been convinced that a mule, when put to it, has as much wit as a philofopher, is fenfible of danger, and takes his precautions to avoid it. Every now and then mine could not avoid kneeling down, as well as his companions; but the muleteers had already warned me not to touch the bridle when that happened, but leave him to himfelf; and I conformed ftrictly to their injunctions, as otherwife I had probably thrown him on his fide, and occafioned fome great mifchief both to the poor animal and to myfelf. However I muft fay that the heavy rains, fallen fome days before, had rendered the way much worfe than we fhould have found it after an interval of dry weather.

It was near ten at night when we reached the *Venta*, where we expected to find fome reft after the fatigue of croffing that plain: but, as ill-luck would have it, there was neither room for us, nor for our mules, becaufe a large

gang

gang of muleteers had already taken poffeffion of it; fo that, we were obliged to go three leagues further to *Orduña*, as there was no place nearer.

The road from the *Venta* to *Orduña* begins with a pafs about ten feet wide, and two hundred long, which is cut thro' a rock, and is fuppofed to have been a work of the Romans. The fides of that pafs are about thirty foot high, as far as I could judge through the obfcurity of the night, and appeared quite perpendicular. At the iffue of the pafs a defcent begins, much fteeper as I thought, than any of thofe on each fide the *Mount Cenis*, or any other mountain I ever croffed before. We came down that fteepnefs along a path made in a zig-zag way. The zig-zags were very fhort at beginning, and the narrow path fo clofe to the edges of a precipice, that woe to us who were riding, if any of our mules had miffed a fingle ftep. This was horrible; and the fnow that covered the top of the mountain, did not mend the matter, as it rendered the ground flippery, though on the other hand, it afforded some light. However, as we advanced, the zig-zags lengthened, the path enlarged gradually, and the ground became clear of the snow; so that, after the first half league there was no further danger to be apprehended from the precipices, and in about four hours we found ourselves below the frightful mountain, marched along a stony plain for an hour more, and happily reached *Orduña* by three o'clock in the morning.

'Tis needless to say, that I was half dead with weariness and cold when we reached the posada. Without assistance I had not been able to alight from my mule; but assistance was not wanting, thanks to the good people of that house, who did all they could to restore me and my companions to the use of our limbs. My companions the Biscayans, I mean;

because

because as to the muleteer and his two men, they had kept themselves warm with walking all the way by our sides, and holding the mules by their halters; besides they are stout mortals, used to go through the greatest fatigues, and to encounter all sort of weathers from their childhood.

The posada at *Orduña* was luckily one of the best I met with in Spain, and I got a bed in it tolerably soft, which was what I wanted most. However, I found myself still so weary in the morning when the muleteer came to receive my orders for our departure, that I could scarcely stir. I therefore discharged him presently, that I might not retard his setting out; and came to a short resolution to stop there two or three days, not only with an intention to rest, but also to see whether I could obtain any kind of interesting information with regard to the language, learning, and antiquities of Biscay, of which *Orduña* is considered as the capital town.

Together with the muleteer and his men, my friend the barber quitted me; but the carpenter defired that he might ſtay to be my interpreter, and I thankfully accepted his offer.

I have already imparted to the reader in the foregoing letters what little knowledge I have been able to pick up at Orduña, and in ſome other parts, with reſpect to the Baſcuenze-language. I have taken likewiſe ſome little notice of the nature of the country, and ſaid ſomething of the ways and manners of the inhabitants. My accounts of Biſcay, and of the other Spaniſh provinces I have viſited, are far from having the degree of perfection that every ſenſible man could wiſh; but I have done what I could, and he gives much who gives all that he can give. Some other traveller, better provided with money, ſenſe, and activity than I, may hereafter undertake the ſame journey, and render this account of mine uſeleſs, by producing a more diſtinct

and

and comprehensive narration. As for me, I have nothing else to add, but that in a few years the way from *Bilbao* to *Madrid* will be rendered more easy and pleasant than I found it, as the Biscayans are actually making a noble road, which is to go from *Bilbao* to *Osina,* without crossing over the horrible *Peña* of *Orduña,* and the not less dangerous territory of *Berberaña.*

INDEX

TO THE

FIRST VOLUME.

LETTER I.

NOTICE given of the departure, Page 1
L. II. *People in the stage coach. Salisbury and its Cathedral. Militia. Bonelace and ducking-stool at* Honiton. *Love whence arising*, 3
L. III. *Fine dressing not blameable. Fifty broken noses. A promise to write trifles*, 13
L. IV. *Manufactures of serges and tapestry. Father* Norbert *and his workmen from France*, 17
L. V. *A man of war and a dock visited*, 22
L. VI. *Fortifications. Mount Edgecombe. An habitation fit for* Jean-Jaques. *An antiquarian and his daughter*, 27
L. VII. *Petty tyranny scarcely avoidable. Incessant rain*, 39
L. VIII. *Chivalry-books. Variations of speech: Tin, gold, and coal-mines in Italy. Why should we work hard?* 43
L. IX. *Pilchards. Packet-boats, and last farewell to England*, 53
L. X. *Sea-sickness. Monsieur or the dog. Neither fight nor storm. Englishmen mending*, 57

L. XI.

INDEX.

L. XI. *Acquaintance contracted at sea. A bag-pipe. Juno's and Venus's,* 76

L. XII. *Tedioufness. Vain efforts to drive it away,* 72

L. XIII. *A* Bonito *and* Flying-fish. *Sea-voyages. Machinery in Epic Poets,* 78

L. XIV. *Life led in a Packet. The beneficial effects of a dinner. Several thousand reis are no riches,* 85

L. XV. *Beauty of a night at sea. Three ships purfuing,* 92

L. XVI. *A hole in the cabbin why and what for,* 95

L. XVII. *Vain-wishes, or castle-building. Study hard. Pronounciation how attained. The rock, the rock,* 100

L. XVIII. *Navigation ended. Batiste and Kelly. Plunge or pay. Banks of the Tagus,* 107

L. XIX. *Pretty Polly's marriage. Bull fight at* Campo Pequeno. *Lufitanian pick-pockets. Dwarfish men and women,* 117

L. XX. *Effects of the earthquake. A city not to be rebuilt in haste,* 137

L. XXI. *The laying of a fundamental stone. A patriarchal pomp. Pied-horfes,* 150

L. XXII. *Another fine prospect. Rhyme and blank-verse. Heavenly life at the Jeronimites. Banks of the Tagus again. Sowing of salt,* 163

L. XXIII. *A specimen of poetical style. An aqueduct,* 178

L. XXIV. *Lapidation performed in a valley. Good workers,* 184

L. XXV. *Good nuns. A scheme for rendering girls still more amiable. Heroism of a young lady,* 191

L. XXVI.

INDEX.

L. XXVI. *Italian Capuchins. Odd fiſhes,* 201

L. XXVII. *A ſhort excurſion. Sad accommodations. Thanks to Aurora,* 212

L. XXVIII. *Promontorium Lunæ. Holes, and Holes, and Holes again. An odd evening walk. A chearful dinner. Coins dropp'd to a Mary Magdalen for a very good reaſon,* 218

L. XXIX. *Vaſt many teeth a going in a great houſe. Genealogical books. The excellence of a circular figure. Gallantry of a devout King,* 230

L. XXX. *No learning in a ſecond life. Ignorance of knowing men. Organs and Clock-work. Mooriſh ornaments,* 248

L. XXXI. *People forbidden to talk. Robbers and not murtherers. Concuſſion from eaſt to weſt. Barraca's. Blacks and their progenies. Jews and their perverſeneſs. Creaking of wheels,* 260

L. XXXII. *An ignorant dialogue. Parade of knowledge. Jeſuits way of teaching,* 281

L. XXXIII. *Fleas, rats, and other conveniencies. Love in one place and liberty in another. Devotion here and devotion there,* 293

INDEX

TO THE

SECOND VOLUME.

LETTER XXXIV.

SLOWNESS *of mules. Yago and Dom Ma-*
nuelo. A defart. Eftalhages, *alias* Stables.
*Female coynefs. The conquering barber. Fools
and thieves,* Page 1

L. XXXV. *An adventure in a wildernefs. Names
of great towns. Ufelffnefs of lyes. An honeft
curate. Pack-faddle-ftuff to invite fleep,* 13

L. XXXVI. *No botanift. Mafquerades and their
various wit. Pictures drawn with the pen.
Pretty dancing. A proclamation,* 20

L. XXXVII. *A military cuftom. Whifkers. A
palace. No travellers expected. A bog-fly. Fine
dancing and fine eyes,* 35

L. XXXVIII. *Love-matters, white cows, a car-
dinal, an old friend and a Portuguefe letter,* 50

L. XXXIX. *A leffon to itinerant writers,* 74

L. XL. *A fketch of the adventures of a Lady.
Come to fee the watch. Talaverolan Poetry,* 81

L. XLI. *Tedioufnefs of uniformity. Leander.
Melon-feeds. General Muza,* 89

L. XLII. *An odd Colonel and a kind Curate.
Boys and girls jumping at my quartillos,* 95

L. XLIII. *Heaps of ftones with croffes. An odd
way of compofing infcriptions. A brave Englifh
girl,* 107

L. XLVI.

INDEX.

L. XLIV. *A tumble-down-hill.* Borracho or Bota, 114

L. XLV. *Much to be seen. Countries most fertile in authors. The question of the edict discussed. Would they cut canals. Virtue wants a rub. Alms-boxes. Sweet-smelling plants. Goats and sheep. No wheat-land,* 117

L. XLVI. Marked by mistake XXXIX. *Flat ground again. Holy friars and pretty girls. Chewing of acorns. An odd organ. Widows lighting candles. Stuff and stuff when I have nothing else,* 134

L. XLVII. *Hogs in numbers. A Spanish Countess. A fellow still sober, and the pistol lost,* 142

L. XLVIII. *Another ugly affair. Silk and earthen manufactures. A dialogue with a* Corregidor, *and a new Calessero,* 158

L. XLIX. *Extempore poetry. Observations upon travelling gentlemen. Towns grow thicker,* 178

L. L. *A Cathedral grand and rich. An Alcazar. The Mozarabic rite. Ximenes's deeds. Abulcacim's history. A brass giant in a cave. A Synagogue. Charles V and Navagero,* 196

L. LI. *Political meditations,* 221

L. LII. *A charming spot. The* Jardinier Sçavant. *Busts ancient and modern. Ladies well behaved. A Theatre. The adventures of the green bird. A pretty village,* 230

L. LIII. *Trifles, such as travel, and such as life supply,* 250

L. LIV. *A stinking town that gives strangers the head-ach.* Locanda *means an* Inn. *Instructions to travellers who happen not to be overloaded with money,* 254

L. LV.

INDEX.

L. LV. *A cunning queen. The palace almost finished. Confidence in priests. A vast many pictures, and why. Missals like Atlas's. Neither grave, nor over-civil, nor reserved, nor jealous. A* Tertulia *is a pretty thing. Leave* alla Spagnuola. *Rice* a la Valenciana 271

L. LVI. *Churches, convents, nunneries, hospitals. Queen* Barbara's *chief passions.* Basquiña *and* Mantilla. Capas *and* Sombreros. *Santa Hermandad. Lists of prohibited books.*
300

INDEX

TO THE

THIRD VOLUME.

LETTER LVII.

ALL men alike. Booksellers and printers. Character of the Spanish language. Spanish Dictionary. Spanish Etymologist. Góngora, Lope de Vega, *and* Calderon. Autos Sacramentales *and* Loas. *The devil in various Plays. The devil turned preacher.* Augustin Moreto. *Not acts, but days. Unities little minded.* Sainete, Zarzuela, Entremés, *and* Mociganga. *The Parish-clerk. Translations of the Classicks, and books of Chivalry.* Quevedo, Feyjoo,

INDEX.

Feyjoo, De L' Isla, *and his* Fray Gerundio. Casiri's *Account of Arabick books.* Juan *and* Ulloa. Lopez. *Public Libraries,* 1

L. LVIII. *A rich town and why. A long conversation with a Lady.* Via Crucis. Año's, Estrecho's, *and* Santo's. *An affecting separation of friends.* 92

L. LIX. *Royal Academy of painting. A fee refused. The private life of a great king.* Farinelli *the famous singer. Women sitting before a royal palace. Mules instead of horses to carriages. Harmlessness of the lower people.* Jubilados, Calessin, *and other matters,* 115

L. LX. *Blind men singing and playing. The* Majo's *dress. Carnival diversions. A description of the new Amphitheatre. Three hundred couples dancing at a time. Strange effect of the* Fandango. *Phrases of address.* Guardias de Corps. Guardias Alabarderos. *Garrison of* Madrid. *Tables of the poor. Tables of the rich. Fish from* Valencia. *Wood for fuel and charcoal. Premature marriages, and why. Burials. Pictures exhibited by preachers. Gripes and bad teeth,* 149

L. LXI. *Squares in every town to fight bulls in. Cruelty inherent in man. A charitable woman. Small chapels by the side of high roads. Colleges ruined, or going to ruin,* 176

L. LXII. *Productions of some Spanish provinces. The life of a muleteer. River* Nares. *Cloth manufactory at* Guadalaxara. *A French* Cook. Hermita *in a Valley with an Inscription on it, &c.* 189

L. LXIII. *A dialogue between a traveller and an ass-driver. The urbanity of a grandee The highest*

INDEX.

highest top in Spain. Cheap rent of houses, 200
L. LXIV. by mistake marked LXI. *Good accounts not to be written from small places. Industrious country-women. Some extempore singing. No such thing among the Arabs,* 213
L. LXV. *Many ruined castles, and why. A French pilgrim. Absurd waste of wax. A Spanish Eunuch,* 219
L. LXVI. *Barren country. Shrubs that serve for fuel. A* Pochero. *A lonely place. English and Spanish dogs. A plant of thyme pluck'd up, and why.* Don Diego, *and his little daughter.* Garnache, *an excellent wine,* 227
L. LXVII. *Sheep-walks in Spain. A vulgar error in Piedmont about mutton.* Don Diego's *manner of travelling. Simplicity of the few inhabitants at* Maria. *A new acquaintance from* Siguenza. *A monarch's supposed schemes. Idleness of people's hopes under a new reign. A gate missed. Two cathedrals in a town. The ugly adventures of* Antonio Perez. *Observations on imperfect rhyming,* 239
L. LXVIII. *Ugliness miraculous, with a guess at the reason of it. Particoloured tiles. Slow travelling advantageous. Churches and other buildings at* Zaragozza. *Pictures representing martyrs. Spanish and Piedmontese Lawyers not to be admired. Painted statues. The idle and the poor equally resort to noted sanctuaries. A country lass kissed by surprise. Blank verse and Assonancies, &c.* 274
L. LXIX. *Wisdom of travel-writers. Character of the Aragonians. Ambition and* Interest, *how called by the Spaniards. Dancing a harmless pastime. People work that can work. Sun and land*

INDEX.

land nearly useless without water. Industry of the Biscayans and Asturians. Why Aragon is more fertile than New Castile. Arrieros, and their manner of life. Variety of pronunciations. The Canon is right in my opinion. Satyrical and bucolic poets, why not hurtful, though they lye. A small desart. The rent of a Venta. *Virtue ill-lodged. Knitting women.* 291

INDEX

TO THE

FOURTH VOLUME.

LETTER LXX.

*D*ESARTS *not frightful. A* Nota Bene *and a* Digression. *Fine faces in Biscay. Great Coquettes. Knowledge of Languages in women.* Landes *of* Bourdeaux. Païs *de* Bigorre. Filles Gasconnes *and* Filles Basquoises. *Biscayans not beggars, and why Many of them at Madrid. They retire to their country. Not so the gentry of Scotland or Savoy. Well-looking houses in Biscay. Dialects of the* Bascuenze. *Laramendi's Works.* Bascuenze-library *small enough. An Irish Merchant at* Bilbao. *Terrifying hills. Wisdom of mules.* Town *of* Orduña, Peña *of* Orduña, *and* River Orduña. *Iron Manufactories.* Chacolín *of* Serraos. *A tool like an* H, *and its use.* Lino, *turkey corn, goats-cheese and milk, small cattle, few sheep, and good pork. Trees*

Vol. IV. Y *annually*

INDEX.

annually planted. Angullas. Orduña *and* Bilbao's *fine fituations. Inconveniencies in Spain. No new edicts, no new laws, no tax-gatherers. Arrival of an Italian finger. The quibbles of Spanifh Capuckins,* page 1

L. LXXI. Don Diego *again. An Irifh Officer. Acceptable news. Irifh regiments. A fine country. An odd Picture. Singing and dancing.* 43

L. LXXII. *Too many fleas. Fare you well,* Señor Don Diego. *Vifit paid to an Univerfity. Manners and drefs of the Students in it. A fine road and a good* Venta. *No broken pate,* 48

L. LXXIII. *Dante's Journey. The moft famous Sanctuary in Spain, the hiftory of its origin, and romanticalnefs of its fituation.* Batifte's *obfervations,* 54

L. LXXIV. *Induftry and activity of rufticks. Their piety. A heavy poll. A fteep hill. Vines formed into feftoons. Streets narrow, but well paved,* 67

L. LXXV. *Situation, climate, and price of things at Barcelona. Its harbour, fquare, and citadel,* 76

L. LXXVI. *A new town.* Las Minas *and* Gages *are two brave men,* 81

L. LXXVII. *Knives faftened to the tables. Various manufactures. Plenty of Taylors, and why. A coach hired,* 85

L. LXXVIII. *Politenefs of Cuftom-men. Manner of travelling in Ca alonia. Catalonian Bufkins. Names of the She-mules,* 92

L. LXXIX. *The great mountains are in fight. An adventure which makes room for fome political confiderations. A cool Chriftian,* 96

L. LXXX.

INDEX.

L. LXXX. *An Inn burnt down. Passage through the Pireneans performed by moon-light. Arrival at Perpignan,* 105

L. LXXXI. *A new method adopted. Light mention made of several places,* 113

L. LXXXII. *A spot once favoured by Cesar. An Andalusian Epicurean, and a learned Innkeeper,* 121

L. LXXXIII. *Remains of an Aqueduct. Wisdom of the Romans.* The Madroño. *The Isle of* St. Marguerite. *Situation of* Antibes, 124

L. LXXXIV. *A short but frightful navigation. A dangerous Cobler. Timely assistance. Montalban and* Villafranca. *A fine Valley. Simplicity of a youth from* St. Remo, 131

L. LXXXV. *Gunpowder under water.* Nice *no great rival to* Genoa *and* Leghorn. *Spanish veracity, French lies, and French urbanity,* 143

L. LXXXVI. *A dwarfish Empire and its contents,* 154

L. LXXXVII. *The Chapel singularly adorned. No adventure at sea. Sea geese. Anchises carrying Eneas. Bite not with feeble teeth. Modest women,* 165

L. LXXXVIII. *A felucca set afloat. Few people help'd to their proper stations.* Tonadilla's *sung. A long chain of habitations. A strong fortress,* 174

L. LXXXIX. *The lies of the inn-keepers at* Genoa. *The last stage,* 183

An APPENDIX *for the instruction of those who go the journey to* Madrid *by land,* 189

The road from Perpignan *to* Madrid, 190
The road from Bayonne *to* Vittoria, 198
The road from Bayonne *to* Pamplona, 200
A few Basque-words explained, 202

INDEX.

The road from Pamplona *to* Madrid, *Description of a Spanish play-house,*	245
Military school at Segovia,	251
The road from Madrid *to* Bayonne, *through* Burgos, Bilbao, *and* St. Sebastian,	257
A wolf that was no wolf,	274
The mules smell out a road,	276
My aunt Philip,	277
Another Pope at Venta del Frayle,	282
A Calentadór *is not an old woman,*	283
Get no bad habits,	284
Courtesy of a friar,	286
Udal ap Rhys,	idem.
Burgos' *cathedral,*	287
A coffee-house tariff,	289
An old wicked woman,	292
A Beata,	293
Friars upon the watch,	idem.
Their stories about images,	294
They will break their bows by overstraining them,	295
The alligator's skin,	296
A plentiful supper,	idem.
A couple of rustick maidens,	297
Old Spanish dress,	idem.
Ranks in a Spanish village,	299
A learned curate,	300
Road from Ameyugo to Vittoria,	302
Riscos *and Peñas near Ameyugo,*	idem.
A fire made of fir wood,	303
A fatiguing day's journey,	304
Mules have some wit,	306
The descent from the Peña *of* Orduña,	307
The appendix concluded,	310

END OF THE FOURTH VOLUME.

www.ingramcontent.com/pod-product-compliance
Lightning Source LLC
Chambersburg PA
CBHW030734230426
43667CB00007B/706